Latin America in Caricature

The Texas Pan American Series

# Latin America in Caricature

John J. Johnson

University of Texas Press, Austin and London

The Texas Pan American Series is published with the assistance of a revolving publication fund established by the Pan American Sulphur Company.

Requests for permission to reproduce material from this work should be sent to Permissions, University of Texas Press, Box 7819, Austin, Texas 78712.

Library of Congress Cataloging in Publication Data

Johnson, John J    1912–
    Latin America in caricature.

    (The Texas Pan American series)
    Includes bibliographical references and index.
    1. Latin America—Relations (general) with the United States—Caricatures and cartoons.    2. United States—Relations (general) with Latin America—Caricatures and cartoons.    3. American wit and humor, Pictoriae.    4. Latin America—Foreign opinion, American.    5. Public opinion—United States.    I.  Title.
F1418.J754      301.29'73'08      79-19052
ISBN 0-292-74626-1

For Steven Michael and Sara Christina

# CONTENTS

Acknowledgments    ix

1.  Introduction    3

2.  The Hemisphere as Monolith    29

3.  Latin America as Female    72

4.  The Republics as Children    116

5.  The Republics as Blacks    157

6.  The Latin American Nations as Non-Black Males    210

7.  Social Reform and Militarism    257

8.  Conclusion    311

    Notes    317

    Index    327

# ACKNOWLEDGMENTS

Caroline Ciancutti assisted me immensely during the research stages of this study. Her dedication to the project was unmistakable. Her "reading" of certain of the cartoons established beyond any doubt her remarkable perceptiveness in the field of human relations. I am indeed indebted to her. Had the book developed as it was originally conceived, Margaret Herlin's research on and analysis of stereotypes in elementary and secondary school textbooks would have figured prominently in it. I hope there will be another occasion when her findings can be put to the level of use they so richly deserve. Janet Dubbs was helpful in endless ways when the project was being launched. Michael Gómez, working out of Bolívar House at Stanford, and Avis Poe Trujillo, in Albuquerque, provided invaluable assistance during the wrap-up period.

Two grants from the Institute of American History, Stanford University, helped to finance the research and preparation of the manuscript for submission to the University of Texas Press where, under the watchful eye of Barbara Spielman, it was improved in a number of ways.

# Latin America in Caricature

# 1. INTRODUCTION

This study of United States–Latin American[1] relations over the past century is nontraditional in at least three respects. First, it is concerned exclusively with the United States' interpretations of developments. Second, it emphasizes the human dimension of relationships rather than the customary security, economic, and nationalist aspects; more specifically, it explores those racial, ethnic, and institutional images[2] of Latin America held by the interested minority of the dominant White Protestant element in the United States.[3] Third, it largely forsakes conventional sources in favor of editorial or opinion cartoons[4] appearing in leading periodicals and newspapers.[5]

Any merit that the book may have rests heavily upon the validity of the following assumptions: (a) Mass communications, to achieve their objective of influencing public opinion, at least to a considerable degree, must reflect the realities, beliefs, and psychological needs of the cultures of which they are a part. (b) The "informed public" in the United States is in a position to influence international relations, and its views are therefore important.[6] (c) The informed public's responses to hemispheric problems and situations are conditioned by culturally imposed qualities of character which are reflected in its perceptions and evaluations of realities, and, as a consequence, its images of Latin America tell us more about the psychological characteristics of informed United States citizens than about their contemporaries in Latin America.[7] (d) Adult citizens of the United States, most particularly those in the more privileged sectors,[8] have considered themselves to be an intrinsically superior species and Latin Americans to be an intrinsically inferior species. At times because of their prejudices[9] and at other times because of an apparent felt need to conform to values of their own group, they have been particularly susceptible to those negative images of Latin America proffered by Washington, the schools, the news media, and other disseminators. (e) While overt expressions of racial superiority are tending to disappear in the United States, there are good reasons to believe that underlying prejudices linger emotionally and may be reflected in interactions between Anglo-America and Latin America.[10] (f) Although the inappropriateness of judging the peoples of Latin America by United States standards is increasingly appre-

4  ciated, there nonetheless remains a pronounced propensity to measure Latin American societies in terms of Anglo-American values. (*g*) In most cases a foreign community's image is not earned but is gratuitously thrust upon it.[11] (*h*) However optimistic I may be about the long term, I am far less so about the short term and expect, as a minimum, matrices of conflict to remain at least over the next quarter century.

Historically, the United States has interacted closely with the republics of Latin America, especially those of the Caribbean, Central America (including Panama), Mexico, Venezuela, and Brazil. Industrial development and trade expansion, a major by-product of which has been a decline in self-sufficiency at the local level and an increasing interdependence at the national level, practically guarantee that the future of each part of the hemisphere will be closely affected by the way its interests mesh with the interests of its neighbors. Although the nations of Latin America have been and will remain important to the United States and vice versa, relationships seldom have been salutary. Characteristically, clouds of misunderstanding and suspicion have hung heavily over the hemisphere. Very often what has been of category-one importance for a given country has been of category-two or -three importance for another. Time and again one or the other of the parties involved has perceived, accurately or inaccurately, that one or more of its goals, purposes, or preferences have been threatened by the intentions or activities of the other.

There are no simple or quick explanations of why the United States and Latin America have behaved toward one another the way they have. Scholars, politicians, and the media have historically seen the antagonism arising from security and economic issues. More recently the intensification of nationalism in Latin America and the reluctance of the United States to accept certain of its consequences have attracted increasing attention from those who seek to inform opinion about hemispheric matters.

There is ample reason for the stress that has been placed on security matters as the linchpin for the explanation of or justification for the failure of the United States and its southern neighbors to formulate and support mutually acceptable policies. To say that security, however much the result of irrational fears and frustrations, has been an absorbing concern for the United States public is practically a truism. Defense was at or near the core of each of the United States' traditional diplomatic stances: isolation-ism, freedom of the seas, the Open Door, the peaceful settlement of dis-putes, the Monroe Doctrine, and Pan Americanism. The Caribbean, Cen-tral America, and the Panama Canal have always figured conspicuously in Washington's security strategies, which with very few exceptions have been conceived in Washington and also implemented from there. Post–World War II actions of the United States underscore this point. Although overall relations between the United States and Latin America were per-mitted to deteriorate disastrously after the defeat of the Axis powers, co-operation at the security level continued at the urging, one might almost say the insistence, of Washington. In 1947 the republics agreed (the Rio Treaty) to the principle that an attack on any American state by any other power would be considered as an attack upon them all and that collective means would be taken to repel such aggression. However, formal agree-ments stipulating cooperation in the field of hemispheric security failed to restrain Washington when it considered the nation's security threat-ened. And on three conspicuous occasions since the signing of the Rio Treaty, Washington has chosen to disregard formal commitments to its hemispheric allies. The first was when the Central Intelligence Agency provided Guatemalan refugees with funds, arms, and combat training that made it possible for them to invade their homeland from neighboring Honduras and topple the regime of Jacobo Arbenz Guzmán (1954), who had accepted backing and had received arms from the Soviet bloc coun-tries. The second was the Bay of Pigs incident (1961) when Washington gave financial and moral support to Cuban refugees intent on ousting Fidel Castro. The third was during the Dominican crisis (1965). On that occa-sion President Lyndon B. Johnson ordered troops ashore in the Domini-can Republic to avert the possibility of what he described as a "communist coup." Only after the situation was considered stabilized was the Organi-zation of American States consulted and the participation of its members in the intervention solicited. The three separate actions tend to confirm the proposition that, so far as the United States is concerned, the same principle of national security and assumption of regional hegemony that were used to justify sending marines into Haiti in 1915 continues in force.[12] Thus, the late Senator Wayne Morse of Oregon was close to the mark when in 1961 he fired the accusation that the way the United States had chosen to achieve its strategic goals had made the country's foreign aid programs of the 1950s and early 1960s one of the most stagnant, un-productive, and misrepresented of all federal activities.[13] Now, over two decades later, it can be added that neither the security-aid mix nor its level of achievement has changed significantly.

Economic issues have contested with security concerns for priority in most analyses of hemisphere relations. But if security and economics have shared major attention, the latter has nearly always generated the greater amount of heat. At times the United States' presence in and influence upon the economies of the republics have been assigned such importance as to make the roles of Latin American nationals and domestic capital appear superfluous to an understanding of the area's industrial growth in this century. Although the facts do not seem to warrant such an extreme position, there is abundant evidence that the United States government and private investors have had a profound impact on the economic evolution of the republics.

With private capital and officials in Washington working in cooperation, United States economic inroads in the area, particularly in the Caribbean, Central America, and Mexico, were quickly consolidated after the War between the States. Before World War I the hemisphere was bound together by flourishing markets, and United States entrepreneurs had launched an all-out economic invasion of the republics.[14] Meanwhile, the United States government had become an apprehensive promoter of economic ties to the south and an active guardian—including the use of customs controls and gunboats—of North American investors. Latin Americans, for their part, had become acutely aware of what they viewed as their disadvantageous position in a system that was developing their immature economies unevenly and leaving them at the mercy of the economic systems of Europe and the United States.

Earlier anxieties of the republics about their subsidiary economic role did not prevent the United States from strengthening its economic penetration after Versailles. It was simply a case of the material desires of the Latin American elites winning out over their trepidations about increasing marketing and financial dependence on the "Colossus of the North." The result was that with the war's end the republics turned to a not reluctant Wall Street, and United States investment soared 70 percent during the decade after 1919.

More than at any previous time hemispheric economic relations between 1930 and 1945 were determined by worldwide phenomena: the Great Depression and World War II. Shattering as were those developments, in many respects their impact upon inter-American affairs was limited to abrupt but short-term changes that could be countered by new strategies and improvisation. And when the world returned to "peace" in 1945 the hemisphere's basic economic relationships and the tactics that had guaranteed them in the past held steadfast.[15]

The United States emerged from the war against the Axis powers relatively stronger economically in Latin America than ever before. That fact alone was perhaps not so important or of as much concern to Latin America as was the realization that Washington had determined to use full-scale economic intervention as a means of achieving its objectives abroad. So far as Latin America was concerned, by the early 1960s several public financial agencies had been established and funded primarily with United States capital, and the Alliance for Progress had been initiated. Washington used its economic control of these agencies to regulate grants-in-aid and loans, to buy support against international communism, to stabilize the status quo, and to assist both civil and military regimes that seemed to give promise of being able to control their constituencies.

In recent times the economic dependency of Latin America, excepting Cuba, has continued to give the United States government and private investors choices denied other nations. Accordingly, "understanding" on economic issues has remained more a consequence of the republics formulating developmental strategies acceptable to Washington than of the outgrowth of healthy conflict and balanced compromise. Gunboat diplomacy during the first third of this century was efficacious only against smaller nations; however, the power of the economic veto exercised thereafter has meant that the flow of capital could be regulated in such ways as to influence economic decisions in small and large nations alike. Furthermore, financial intervention evoked fewer objections at home than did the "sending of marines."

Nationalism is generally considered to be the dominant variable in contemporary hemispheric relations. This ideology achieved its current standing only after several decades of change in its character and objectives. Outcries against foreign economic domination before World War I had nationalist overtones but they were muffled largely by export-import sectors in the republics dedicated to bringing their nations into the mainstream of Western democratic capitalism by means of vastly expanded international trade and large influxes of foreign capital and technology. Two consequences of World War I led to the growth of what might be called cultural nationalism: (*a*) the seeming decline of France, to whom Latin America traditionally had looked for cultural guidance, and (*b*) the emergence of the United States, whose culture Latin Americans deeply disdained, as the money capital of the world. The intellectual elites of the republics sought to counter those developments by finding qualities important to national growth within domestic groups who historically had been left to vegetate on the fringes of national life. The Mexican Indianist movement of the 1920s—during which intellectuals from all walks of life, but most particularly anthropologists, artists, and educators, were called upon to rehabilitate native peoples so that they might ultimately justifiably be integrated into society—is one of the better known responses of cultural nationalism to the area's postwar identity concerns.

The intellectuals had not made significant progress when, with the onset of the Great Depression, politicians seized upon the nationalist theme and gave it a strongly populistic coloration and economic orientation. State regulation of wages, hours, and services, tighter restrictions on foreigners in the work force, and protective tariffs were instituted, all designed to appeal to popular elements by providing employment for nationals, retaining within their respective countries a larger portion of the profits of foreign operations, and creating climates in which local industry might supply some of the consumer goods that historically had placed strains on the republics' foreign exchange earnings. The new restrictions soon created heated disputes. In retrospect, one recognizes that foreign investors and managers overreacted to the controls over labor and industry more because of their novelty than their direct impact on production and profits. But, at the time, both sides felt that their futures were at stake.

The antiforeign, anti–North American variants of nationalism were temporarily submerged in the climate of hemispheric unity (seriously strained only by the policies of regimes in Argentina and Bolivia) that prevailed during World War II. By the end of the struggle in Europe, however, more strident nationalism with stronger statist trappings had appeared and was upstaging all other developments in hemispheric relations. The

postwar nationalism was and remains distinctly anti–North American.
And, while retaining the older cries of exploitation, excessive profits, and foreign domination of local governments, the republics have utilized potent forms of nationalist expression against multinational companies, as well as attempting to circumvent Washington's insistence on the maintenance of an anti-Soviet bloc.

United States responses to the more nationalistic directions taken in the post–World War II era proved markedly negative and unaccompanied by serious or constructive proposals. Instead, each and every program emanating from Washington, including the Alliance for Progress, retained for the United States the privilege of formulating the strategies and tactics under which Latin America was theoretically to develop. Not only is such an approach morally arrogant, but it is also doomed to failure on at least two scores: it overlooks the seriously limited capacity of an external agency to influence and reshape an alien culture and it requires a subservience that Latin American nationalists will no longer abide. As a consequence, the nationalistic distrust of United States motives remains as intense as it is constant and the dialectic of misunderstanding and hostility consequently continues unabated.[16]

The above synthesis suggests the relevance that the United States traditionally has attached to its security and economic interests in the Latin American area as well as the salience of nationalism in contemporary hemispheric relations. What the brief review does not adequately explain is (*a*) why, historically, the United States government has claimed the right to assume full responsibility for the defense of the hemisphere south of the Rio Grande and unilaterally to determine if and when military forces should be brought into play; (*b*) why the United States government and private citizens have pursued exploitive tactics in the economic area; or (*c*) why the United States has so strongly opposed the growth of nationalism in Latin America. I believe, and so contend in this volume, that both our public and our private dealings with Latin American republics have resulted to a significant degree from widely accepted stereotyped negative images of their people, religion, and value systems. I further believe and argue herein that our unfavorable stereotypes of Latin America are largely the product of our cultural assumptions.

United States negative images of Latin America, which have been

...anded down from one generation to the next, date from the earliest contacts of the two cultures. Most of them were formalized by 1830 and the remainder by 1860. That the images have had a vigorous life for more than a century, as the succeeding chapters of this volume attest, speaks both to their currency over time and to the conviction with which they have been held. Two basic assumptions originally undergirded the images. The first was that the Black Legend,[17] as it developed in England and was exported to Great Britain's New World possessions, realistically represented the Spanish Catholic character at the time of the conquest and early colonization and that the Spanish personality was unmodified by time. In general that assumption served Hispanophobes well throughout the colonials' struggle against Iberian dominance and during the embryonic years of nationhood, when military and political leadership was a near White European monopoly, and yet again before and during the Spanish-American War. The second assumption was that neither of the two other major racial groups—Native Americans and Blacks—nor the large "mixed" elements measured up even to the lowly regarded Iberians. This latter view first found widespread acceptance during the era of Manifest Destiny, roughly between 1830 and 1850. It was reinforced in the 1850s by certain pseudoscientists who more than compensated for their lack of scientific fact with dogmatic assertion. It finally flowered in the 1890s under the guise of social Darwinism and as a rationalization for expansionism.

The Black Legend faulted the Spaniard in a number of areas that would later be reflected in Anglo-American caricatures of him. The legend held him to be decadent, as evidenced by his rejection of progress and, in the highest levels of State, his acceptance of illegitimacy, incest, and gross neglect of responsibility. It identified him as an authoritarian, as manifested in his belief in imposing government from above, by force if necessary, and ruling by decree. The inevitable legacy of such an approach to government, the argument ran, was either strong-man rule or revolution and discontent. This stereotype appeared to be supported by the widespread use of force to attain power and suppress opposition even before independence was everywhere assured. The legend further found the Spaniard corrupt, a by-product that might be anticipated given his view of government office as a route to personal wealth instead of public service.[18] The legend also held that the Spaniard placed a low value on personal toil; his attitude seemed always to be that if work were worthwhile someone else would have grabbed it long ago. The legend labeled the Iberian as cruel, as demonstrated by the atrocities he perpetrated against the Native Americans in his zeal to spread Roman Catholicism and in his merciless exploitation of the defenseless working man throughout the colonial era.[19] The conduct of General Valeriano "Butcher" Weyler and the treatment of inmates in the Spanish concentration camps in Cuba at the end of the nineteenth century, as reported in the United States press, seemed to furnish overwhelming evidence that the Spaniard had not changed.[20]

For more than any other reason, perhaps, initially the Spaniard invited the wrath of Anglo-America because of the Roman Catholic church and the role he assigned it in his society. His Christianity was early and lastingly typified in the Inquisition, associated in the Protestant mind with the grossest of repression, terror, and torture. His religious were suspect on the grounds that the life of a monk or a nun was no calling because prayer must be personal, not a way for particular individuals to make a living. He joined Church and State in a manner that made every enemy of the State a heretic. His religion was opposed to both intellectual and political liberty and held itself apart from and above the community, while "American" churches were considered to be on the side of the future and against the "papal past." Even by the early nineteenth century in the United States, the term *pope* had become a by-word for provincial bigotry.[21] The Spaniard's religious institution participated in large-scale lending and land-ownership, activities that were incompatible with Anglo-American ideas and institutions. His investment of labor and wealth in elaborate church architecture in Mexico, Peru, and elsewhere was compared unfavorably with the modest investment in houses of worship in the United States.

There were bad Spaniards; no right-thinking person would quarrel with that. But what the Black Legend, as propagated in the United States, did was to make badness inherent in the Spaniard and, as it soon developed, also in his direct heirs, the Creoles.[22] As a result, when Spain and Portugal were expelled from the mainland, not only were old stereotypes transferred to the Creoles, but also new ones were created and nurtured. One such stereotype, that of the elites as ideologically immature, appeared even before independence was achieved. Its substance derived from the fact that many of their numbers initially displayed a strong propensity for monarchical government. And that was a position the republican mind saw as if not unfathomable at least backward looking. The Latin

12  American leaders to this day have not shaken the image of their being ideologically unsophisticated, and when certain governments leaned toward fascism in the 1930s and 1940s and others toward international communism and Castroism in the 1950s, 1960s, and 1970s the image was in fact reinforced. At the same time that they were being found lacking in ideological acumen there was being created an image of them as being socially naïve. This stereotype emerged because of their relative lack of prejudice against colored persons and the readiness of their sovereign assemblies to emancipate African slaves during the independence movements.[23] Still another view that became a well-embedded stereotype had them economically improvident because, among other reasons, they were disinclined to defer immediate pleasures of the moment in favor of the greater good of the morrow. Their widely circulated *mañana* spirit added conviction to Anglo doubts about their future prosperity. Finally, the Creoles were portrayed as unnecessarily dependent on standing armies, institutions thoroughly distrusted by Anglo-Americans as dangerous to their civil liberty and freedom. That image has been kept alive and well and has been a popular target of the cartoonists, as Chapter 7 certifies.

At this point a very important qualification is called for, namely, that the Anglo-American indictment of the Spanish Creole males was not extended to their feminine counterparts. Individuals occasionally found the women to be somewhat shallow and priest ridden, but on the whole my evidence rates them well above their men folk. Reports from United States agents, traders, and adventurers generally stressed the women's physical attractiveness and their taste in dress.[24] Chapter 3 provides telling testimony to the cartoonists' strong preference for female symbolism when they have chosen to create a sympathetic image of Latin America.

Returning now to the central theme, what the Anglo-Americans had done within the single decade of the 1820s was to make themselves the near antithesis of the Latin Americans. And the dichotomy between "we" and "they" persists. The speed with which the sharp distinctions were drawn is largely explainable more by what was occurring in the United States than by activities in Latin America. Increasing contacts, both private and public, between Anglo and Latin America came when change in the United States had never been so extensive. Diplomatic and military triumphs had been won. Newly acquired territories and territories yet to be acquired were being peopled. Everywhere there was extraordinary spatial and social mobility. Conditions being so favorable in the United States, closer associations between north and south proved to a majority of Anglo-American thinkers what they had presumed to be true in the first place rather than upsetting old theories in their long-established intellectual foundations. Even those who depicted the Latin Americans in favorable terms[25] equivocated when the destiny of the Latin American nations was measured against that of the United States. Thus, Anglo-American rationality, pragmatism, temperance, honesty, industry, and frugality—basically a list of virtues drawn from the Puritan ethic, stripped of theological trappings[26]—were juxtapositioned against those negative qualities associated with the Latin Americans; it mattered little which Latin American—Mexican, Venezuelan, Brazilian, Chilean, or whomever—all were assumed to possess the same basic qualities. This is the essential point of Chapter 2. The contest, preceded as it was by this kind of early psychological warfare, was unequal and the outcome predictable, if for no other reason than that the rules of the game were decided unilaterally by rule makers suffering from acute cultural myopia.[27] In the knowledge that their own revolution was catching fire, they breathed a confidence understood at the time only by themselves.[28] Little wonder that they gave minimal thought to the possibility that there is no satisfactory criterion as to what constitutes a superior culture.

In terms of hemispheric relations, it is interesting to speculate on what the consequences might have been had Anglo-America "discovered" Latin America at a time when greater value would have been assigned to similarities instead of differences in the two cultures, for the similarities covered a broader range of attitudes and values than is generally appreciated. Both peoples, for example, viewed future European colonialization in the New World in essentially the same terms. They both favored a "limited" state whose primary role over and beyond defense against foreign enemies was the enhancement of individualism through internal order and the protection of private property. And their concepts of private property were less differentiated than the relative size of private holdings in the two areas would suggest. Also, the practice of strictly limiting the electoral franchise was common to both societies, the assumption being that the property holder was an adequate repository for the suffrage because the best interests of the community were represented in him. Each culture saw institutionalized religions as a social stabilizer. In each

14 culture State and Church cooperated in attempts to acculturate native peoples. And both peoples supported an elite educational philosophy that placed great emphasis on cultural continuity.

However, not only were similarities discounted, but also differences were accentuated as the Mestizos (persons of "mixed" European and Indian heritage) almost immediately challenged "White" rule in several of the mainland nations extending from Mexico to Bolivia, and in the United States, Manifest Destiny gripped the imagination of Anglo-America. In its most strident form during the 1830s and 1840s, Manifest Destiny was a psychological mixture of predestination, religion, optimism, and exaggerated nationalism. Its postulates were that (*a*) Anglo-Saxons are endowed as a race with innate superiority over other races, (*b*) Protestant Christianity holds the key to heaven, (*c*) only republican forms of government are free, (*d*) liberal institutions offer the chance and individualism the motive for success, and (*e*) the future can be hurried along by human hands.[29] Manifest Destiny thus in affect made White people the model for the human race, and to the degree that other humans differed from the model so much would they be judged to have inherited more of the qualities which ordinarily would preclude their escaping the limits of their civilization. Philosophically, the presumed superiority of the Anglo-Saxon population and republican institutions of the United States quickly ushered in a strong sense of "mission," a civilizing burden. The "American" people were overwhelmed with a Christian obligation to "regenerate" less advantaged peoples. Practically, the ideology initially provided an essentially cultural justification for territorial expansion, domestically against Native Americans, internationally against Mexicans, and ultimately as a patronizing view toward all Latin Americans and Pacific islands peoples as well.

Mexico, whose active population was already primarily Mestizo, felt the impact of Manifest Destiny, first in Texas during the 1830s and there and elsewhere by the late 1840s. Anglo migrants in Texas, after living side by side with the original Mexican settlers for a decade, concluded that they were the degenerate, revolutionary progeny of racially different parents who had inherited not a redeeming feature of the Indian and the worst qualities of the Spaniard. The targeting of the Mestizos as one of the low points of human society amounted to substituting them for the Indians as the negative reference point in the Anglo Protestant's age-old con-

cern about individual morality, family life, and cultural integrity in the
New World's wilderness environment.[30] Once the idea of the Mestizo as a
negative prototype found acceptance, it quickly gained currency. The
attention the Mestizos attracted was due in large part to the fact that the
Native Americans could no longer be considered a worthy foe against
which to wage cultural warfare. Generally removed from their lands east
of the Mississippi, their attacks on White communities subsiding, seen as
representing undefined lost values, and, according to the prevailing wisdom, doomed to extinction, the Indians, far from being an object of scorn,
were rapidly becoming eligible for the sentimental nostalgia commonly
accorded vanquished peoples.[31]

The low regard in which the Mestizo was held following the United
States–Mexican War raised what must remain an unanswerable question:
To what extent, if any, did the fact that Mexico's population was five-sixths
*gente de color*—Indians, Mestizos, Blacks, and Mulattoes—figure in the
United States decision not to absorb all of Mexico (and perhaps Central
America as well) in the 1840s? Certainly there were individuals in high
positions who wondered aloud about such a "mixture." Could it ever be
regenerated? If it could be, how long would it take? In the meantime, what
should be the status of those people? What effect would admitting them
to United States citizenship have on "American" institutions? And how
might the "All Mexico" element, who would bestow the blessings of
"American" order, peace, and freedom upon their benighted Mexican
brethren, have fared had the "New England conscience" been able to
subordinate the moral problem of slavery, and its extension, to the getting
of land?[32]

The Mestizos never recovered from their early victimization. Wher-
ever they constituted a significant share of the population, and in some
places where they did not, they became and for the most part have remained the "sombreroed, lazy, improvident, ungovernable, revolutionary" who, in the dominant North American thinking, has kept the nations
of Latin America from becoming "modern" stable societies. Their ubiqui-
tousness to a considerable degree explains why in the succeeding pages
Mestizo types appear often and the stereotypical Indian only randomly.

There seems to be no such thing as an "all-duty scapegoat" and the
Mestizo has been no exception. As it turned out, they came to share that
role with their Black and Mulatto compatriots. Although Anglo-America

16    historically has claimed a profound concern for all of Latin America, the truth is that its interests, whether political, economic, or intellectual, have been concentrated in the Caribbean and its periphery and Brazil. This was especially true until the 1930s when United States hegemony in the hemisphere came under attack, first from fascism, then from communism, and more recently from Latin American varieties of nationalism. And it was in and around the Caribbean and in Brazil that Latin America's Black population was concentrated. More particularly, in several of the countries, for example, Mexico, Colombia, and Venezuela, Blacks centered on the coasts, including the ports frequented by Yankee traders and naval personnel. As a consequence, during the century that the United States showed little other than economic and security interests in Latin America, its population was commonly reported to be comprised of Blacks, with no distinction being made between them and the Mulattoes.[33]

Being identified as Black in the Anglo-American folk wisdom augured badly for the peoples of Latin America. At home Blacks had been stripped of virtually all the rights accorded to White settlers under common law.[34] The few Whites who explicitly denied a belief in White superiority generally betrayed a deeper conviction, namely, that the Black was inferior to the White. Those in the White community opposed to slavery avoided the issue of equality. By the middle of the nineteenth century, anxieties over real and potential slave uprisings were increasingly incorporated into the thinking that had raised genuine, if unfounded, doubts concerning the Blacks' inherent fitness for freedom and the prospects of their incorporation into White society on equal terms.[35]

As the abolitionist debate heated, proslavery forces discovered a "scientific" justification for their beliefs in "craniology," the study of the size of the brain, the shape of the skull, and the nature of suture. Samuel George Morton, the leader of the school in the United States, and his disciples concluded that the skulls of various races ranged considerably in size, the largest belonging to Caucasians. To them that proved conclusively the superiority of the White and the inferiority of the Black races,[36] the substructure on which envenomed racism was built.

Racism[37] gained added momentum in the 1860s when Darwinian biology was popularized and its potentialities as a rationale for racist attitudes became apparent.[38] By subsuming mankind wholly under the grim

physical laws of the animal kingdom it confirmed for many that ascent up
the ladder of social evolution was closely linked to mental capacity, which
was assumed a function of cranial size. Under the dual influences of craniology and Darwinism, White supremacy became the comprehensive philosophy of life that it would remain for the next three decades.[39]

White supremacy, Darwinism, and unsurpassed technological progress gave impulse to two currents of racial nationalism by the 1890s, one
defensive and directed against the foreigner within, the other aggressive
and calling for expansion overseas. The latter at best led to paternal despotism and at worst to the United States employing extraordinary and
sometimes coercive means, especially in Latin America, to reshape the international, political, economic, and social structures of sovereign communities.[40] In the conviction that it had found the key to order and progress, on no less than twenty separate occasions between 1898 and 1920
United States marines or soldiers entered the territories of the states in the
Caribbean.[41]

After 1900 racial demagogy declined in intensity, but it would not go
away. As distinguished a scholar as Edward Ross, intermittent nativist with
fervent populist-progressive views and generally recognized as one of the
fathers of sociology in the United States, used the tenets of racism as psychological ammunition in his defense of controls upon immigrant workers and in justification of the traditional social-economic middle groups
retaining their cultural hegemony.[42] Many social issues at the local, state,
and national levels continued to be stated in Black-White terms through
the 1920s when the idea of cultural pluralism provided a new context for
conceptions of cultures and cultural relativity.[43] Chapter 5 makes clear
that any changes for the better between 1900 and 1930 went unnoticed
by the cartoonists who freely employed the physical and verbal stereotypes associated with southern Blacks as a way of communicating their
views of the peoples of Latin America.

Gunnar Myrdal, commenting on race relations between Blacks and
Whites in the 1940s, noted that, while racism as a comprehensive ideology was still maintained by only a few, prejudice as an attitude remained
common.[44] The limited empirical evidence dating from the 1920s indicates that Myrdal's assessment of White prejudices against Blacks could
have been applied more or less equally to Latin Americans. There was no

longer an encompassing ideology, such as Manifest Destiny or racism, that relegated Latin Americans to inferior status but prejudice against them clearly persisted in the 1940s as it did before and after that date.

As early as 1928, sociologist Emory S. Bogardus found, when he gave a series of 140 questions designed to measure social distance to a sample of 1,725 respondents representing a cross section of the United States public, that only 28 percent would have admitted Mexicans to close kinship by marriage while 15.1 percent favored totally excluding Mexicans from entering the United States.[45] In another investigation of racial prejudices Bogardus asked 110 businessmen and schoolteachers on the Pacific Coast about degrees of social intimacy and found that Mexicans ranked seventeenth in a preferential rating of twenty-three ethnic groups, being favored over Chinese, Japanese, Negroes, Mulattoes, Hindus, and Turks.[46]

More recent and perhaps more sophisticated polls confirmed Bogardus' findings. On December 10, 1940, the Office of Public Opinion Research conducted a nation-wide poll in which respondents were given a card with nineteen words on it and were asked to indicate those words that seemed to describe best the people of Central and South America. The results were as follows:

| | | | |
|---|---|---|---|
| Dark-skinned | 80% | Imaginative | 23% |
| Quick-tempered | 49% | Shrewd | 16% |
| Emotional | 47% | Intelligent | 15% |
| Religious | 45% | Honest | 13% |
| Backward | 44% | Brave | 12% |
| Lazy | 41% | Generous | 12% |
| Ignorant | 34% | Progressive | 11% |
| Suspicious | 32% | Efficient | 5% |
| Friendly | 30% | No answer | 4% |
| Dirty | 28% | No opinion | 0% |
| Proud | 26% | | |

Since respondents were asked to pick as many descriptive terms as they liked, percentages add to considerably more than 100.[47]

If dark-skinned and religious (read Catholic) can be considered negative images, as they unquestionably were in pre–World War II United States, then the respondents showed preference for eight unfavorable terms—dark-skinned, quick-tempered, emotional, religious, backward, lazy, ignorant, suspicious—as descriptive of Latin America before recording a favorable one—friendly—and returning to a negative one—dirty— as their tenth choice. It is no less significant that the lowest score was registered for "efficient," which figures so prominently in the Protestant ethic.

A Gallup poll conducted in 1968 reveals attitudes not unlike those of the prewar years. Respondents were asked to rate twenty-eight nations, five of which were Latin American republics: Brazil, Argentina, Chile, Uruguay, and Cuba. (The method used was the Shapel Scalometer consisting of ten squares or boxes numbered from plus five to minus five.) In the very favorable ratings (plus fives and plus fours combined) Canada, with 64 percent, was ranked the highest. Brazil, rated very favorable by 13 percent of the respondents, tied with Israel for fifteenth in the rank ordering; Argentina, favored by 11 percent, ranked eighteenth; Chile, with 8 percent, tied with India for the twentieth position; Uruguay, with 7 percent, was rated twenty-second; and Cuba, with less than 1 percent, tied with Communist China for the last position. Cuba excepted, all of the Latin America republics were rated above Iran, Egypt, Russia, North Vietnam, and Communist China but not above any "Western" nation.[48]

In summary, at the top of the list of those qualities that have influenced our views of the republics to the south go our racial attitudes and associated sentiments, born of a combination of emotionalism, biological taboos, and hereditarian determinism. Those attitudes and the resultant prejudices have been so much a part of our collective thought processes that it can be argued that the strategies used by individuals and public and private agencies sympathetic to the area and its underprivileged populations may actually reinforce in the United States those images of the republics that historically have worked to their disadvantage. The reasoning is as follows. Missionary welfare groups, such as CARE, make their case for support on the grounds of poverty and/or technological backwardness, the supposed beneficiaries almost always pictured as Indian or Black or "mixed" types. While such a presentation, for whatever reason, apparently is considered effective in seeking philanthropic aid, it tends to lend credence to the popular impression of Latin America as peopled by dark-hued and, it follows, "inferior races," unable or unwilling to help themselves.

The religious views of the historically dominant elements in the United States likewise had the effect of placing Latin America in a disadvantageous position. The republics were Roman Catholic or "papist"; the

20    United States, at least through the 1920s, was staunchly and combatively Protestant. Protestant literature and standard public school textbooks depicted the Catholic clergy as so grossly ignorant and bigoted as to disqualify it as a standard-bearer of either Christian ethical standards or acceptable cultural values. Those Protestants who questioned the prevailing view were left to search out for themselves evidence of the Church's contribution in the fields of education, science, hospital care, and philanthropy, in each of which it was the central institution throughout Latin America until replaced by the State, a phenomenon of the recent past. If in the last several decades United States Protestants have tempered their views toward Catholicism, it remains a fact that a large share of the classroom literature on Latin America has continued somehow to link Catholicism with the "backwardness" of the republics.[49]

Finally, Latin America's political institutions, which in practice generally have not conformed to the United States model, have served to cast the area in an unfavorable light. Educated to worship democracy founded on faith in the power and courage of free men, the United States public in general has remained firm in the conviction that their style of democracy, despite its failure to provide answers to all the issues born of industrialization and urbanization or to prevent periodic eruptions of class warfare, is superior to political systems in other parts of the world. Given this faith in their perceived experience, it is perhaps not surprising that they have attempted to export democracy to Latin America, which has seemed to enjoy few of the benefits closely associated with responsible government in the United States. Thus, the tendency of the informed public, either out of ignorance or out of conviction, has been to deny credence to alternative traditions and values which may be ill-suited to "democracy" as comprehended in the United States. As a consequence, they gave unquestioning approval to the Good Neighbor Policy in the 1930s and 1940s and the Alliance for Progress in the early 1960s, one of whose major goals was the creation of vital centers in Latin America where a political style fashioned after the United States political pattern would take root and flourish and thereby save Latin America from itself.[50]

There is nothing original about calling attention to the United States' low esteem, when not scorn, for Latin Americans and their institutions. Throughout our history we have been aware that we have been prejudiced unfavorably toward and have discriminated against the people of the various republics. What is perhaps more significant and certainly less often reported is that at no time have we as a society seemed aware that, to the degree our array of ascribed features of Latin America has been actually and philosophically false, it has been unrealistic to expect lasting understanding. Rather we have acted so as to give the impression that immediate gains have been worth the risk of disparaging the peoples and institutions of the republics so long as the consequences did not lead to the immediate collapse of hemispheric relations.

Initially, it was my intent to establish what have been the racial, ethnic, and institutional images of Latin America in the minds of knowledgeable elements in the United States as those images have been revealed in a variety of commonly employed historical sources. In pursuit of that goal I began by examining in some depth diplomatic correspondence of the nineteenth century, especially communications to the State Department from agents in the field and congressional debates. I then turned to memoirs of public officials with experience in Latin America during the early decades of this century. Later, I researched missionary journals and field reports of churchmen covering the period from 1850 to 1920, public school and college textbooks as well as scholarly evaluations of their factual and ideational content,[51] the mass media, and public opinion polls. As the project progressed it became quite apparent to me that cartoonists whose art was appearing in leading publications were capsulizing and marketing to the reading public nearly all the images of Latin America being perpetuated by public officials, missionaries, editors, publishers, and textbook authors and being reflected in the public's responses to social surveyors and professional pollsters. It seemed equally clear to me that cartoonists were recording opinions in a way at least as likely to fix or reinforce impressions in the public mind as were their contemporaries who were depending upon the printed word. I therefore determined to shift my attention almost exclusively to editorial cartoons on the grounds that they would tell the story more concisely and with greater clarity than would the broad range of traditional sources.[52]

Reliance upon editorial cartoons as a prime documentary source raises at least four problems, two of which may be termed substantive and two methodological. The first substantive issue relates to the reliability of cartoons. They are, of course, drawn by artists who make no pretense of presenting the whole truth. On the contrary, cartoonists have a reputation for taking liberties with or oversimplifying the facts in order to make their intent evident. Once at their drawing boards they become first and foremost advocates who invite their viewers to join them in acceptance of policies they favor. The essence of cartooning is attack to the point where heroes are glorified by denouncing their adversaries. As a consequence, a cartoon can be and often is a fundamental distortion of a reality. It tells either more than the truth or less than the truth. Perhaps more seriously, there is no place in a cartoon for reasoned criticism or detailed argument, much less an opportunity to develop a philosophical position. By its very nature, then, a cartoon lends itself to "one side of the story" and has no place for an outline of the converse picture that we have a right to expect in dispassionate scholarly exposition.

The second substantive problem arises from the fact that cartoons are essentially little more than tangible expressions of established myths. By design they exploit the unreflective fusion of the metaphysical and symbolic through the use of reiteration and sensationalism. And on those occasions when cartoons treat issues involving two or more nations, there is added to the above the very present realization that they mythologize the world of international relations by physiognomizing it. They thereby contribute to the all too evident tendency of individuals to think of political sovereignties not as political sovereignties but as persons.[53] I concluded that, since this study would not be concerned, first of all, with the historical accuracy of cartoon reporting on hemisphere matters but rather with the opinions and symbols that cartoonists tapped to elicit an immediate and favorable public response, the ever-present possibility that such cartoons grossly misrepresent the realities of a given situation would not minimize their importance, indeed would accentuate it.

The methodological problems raised in using cartoons as historical documentation are of more consequence. In the first place, valid and reliable data relating to the use of cartoons as a means of communication are sharply limited.[54] Lewis James Davies' sociological study of the form and content analysis of the cartoon as a cultural medium of communication attacks the methodological issue with impressive data, but his work must be considered introductory.[55] LeRoy Maurice Carl presents limited statistical data suggesting that cartoons may generate quite different meanings among members of a single social-economic group.[56] Carl's conclusion does not necessarily invalidate the idea of a substratum of more general beliefs, values, and so on which condition those responses. The remainder of the literature exploring the significance of cartoons as editorial commentary is based largely on intuition or chance observation and is of quite uneven quality. Notably lacking are data of a psychological nature which explore the processes by which a cartoon becomes part of or reinforces an individual's thought pattern, if in fact that actually occurs.

The second methodological problem is that there are extremely few scholarly data on the extent to which cartoons influence public thinking. The "professional students of caricature," as W. A. Coupe calls them,[57] are in general convinced that cartoonists work a fertile field and harvest abundantly. In some cases one need only note the titles of studies to appreciate the conviction with which the case for cartooning is made. William G. Rogers, for example, entitled his book *The Pen Is Mightier Than the Sword*.[58] Scott Long left little doubt of his view when he entitled one of his articles "The Political Cartoon: Journalism's Strongest Weapon" and then went on to contend that "the political cartoon is still beyond doubt the strongest editorial weapon in the whole arsenal of either right or wrong."[59] In a similar vein and with equal confidence in the cartoonists, Bob Eckhardt entitled an article "The 'Art' of Politics: Why the Pen Is Mightier Than the Meathook."[60]

Those who hold that cartoons have significant editorial clout argue their case from essentially three directions. First, they point out that the impact of cartoons is evidenced by the fact that publishers and editors have kept cartoonists on company payrolls, often as the highest paid members of the editorial staff, and have given their art prominent billing for over two centuries.[61] Second, they seek to establish the importance of cartoons by calling attention to cases of public figures who have stated that cartoons have influenced their careers. Few serious students of cartooning miss the opportunity to recall Thomas Nast's role in destroying the public career of Boss Tweed in New York City.[62] Walter Lippmann stated without equivocation in 1931 that the feelings of protest and outrage in the 1920s found their best expression in the cartoons of Rollin Kirby of *New York World*. Historian Allan Nevins declared unequivocally that cartoonists swayed many votes in the Blaine-Cleveland election of 1884.[63]

And Eckhardt, choosing to ignore the fact that politicians are often overly generous with their credits, informed his readers that Presidents Ulysses S. Grant and William McKinley believed that their electoral triumphs were greatly aided by the drawings of Nast and the artists of *Judge*.[64] More recently, former President Gerald Ford, on the occasion of viewing a gallery of United States political cartoons, is reported to have observed, "The pen is mightier than the politician."[65] The fact that a relatively few "credits" are cited over and over suggests, however, that the established number of individuals who have publicly conceded that they were either the beneficiaries or the victims of cartoon opinion may be quite small.

The third category of evidence used to support the position that cartoons do influence the observer breaks down into time and sight elements. According to the time argument, cartoons are instant art, the meaning of which strikes through at a glance, while reading an editorial takes time that many readers are unwilling to sacrifice. Cartoons thus become a substitute for some of the ponderous writing that typifies many editorial pages. The sight argument is apparently as old as Confucius and holds that a picture is worth a thousand or ten thousand words, depending upon whom one chooses to cite. Or, to put it another way, a cartoon creates impressions that are believed to survive those fashioned by the printed word.

Only an occasional author has questioned the view that cartoons are effective communicators. Henry Ladd Smith is one such person. He contended that the first quarter of the twentieth century was the golden age of the political cartoonists because issues were comparatively simple and easily interpreted and there was enough elemental violence in them to satisfy the satirist. Influence of the cartoonists, according to Smith, declined in the second quarter of the century because they lost their monopoly of visual entertainment to other art forms, as for example movies and comic strips.[66] The distinguished cartoonist J. N. "Ding" Darling of the *Des Moines Register*, was even more skeptical of the influence that cartoonists have had. He observed, "I doubt that they [cartoons] ever moved any mountains or changed the course of history."[67] Coupe aligns himself with Smith and Darling when he writes in his reflective article, ". . . fortunately . . . in an age of mass communications and general literacy cartoonists do not have the effect on public opinion that professional students of caricature sometimes impute to them."[68] And Frank Whitford strikes from an-

other angle when he insists that individuals look forward to the daily cartoon only for so long as they are not shocked too thoroughly or their own
beliefs are not held up to too much ridicule.[69]

Those who have been more conservative in their judgments about
the degree to which cartoons may shape or re-enforce public attitudes
stress the economic aspects of publishing. Their position is that only the
very exceptional cartoonists, as for example Thomas Nast at *Harper's
Weekly* and David Low at Lord Beaverbrook's *Evening Standard*, have
been granted an important part in shaping editorial policy because in an
overwhelming number of cases employers have been unwilling to chance
the loss of circulation in the interest of giving their cartoonists freedom of
expression.[70] Also, as cartoonists have become syndicated and appear in
media catering to a variety of views, the tendency to fence-sitting probably has increased.[71] If one accepts that as a group publishers have exercised restraints on editorial opinion, it follows, then, that the vast majority
of cartoonists probably have gravitated to newspapers and journals with
views similar to their own. And if that is true, it would also be true that ( *a* )
most cartoon lecturing is directed to the already converted rather than to
the uncommitted and is designed to arouse the ardor of the reader with
like beliefs and appeals to sentiments well within the context of the viewer's information and knowledge; ( *b* ) political cartoonists draw for a particular kind of reading audience from whom they can expect a certain
amount of support; and ( *c* ) the cartoonist's opportunity to have an impact
is probably less today when newspapers and journals must compete with
other media than it was when they held a virtual monopoly on the public's
attention and quest for news and opinion.[72] This line of argument leads to
a point crucial to this study: namely, that cartoonists have been less opinion shapers and more buttresses of existing opinions.

I believe that the particular nature of this project obviates all of the
more serious problems generally associated with the use of cartoons as
historical evidence. The likelihood that cartoonists follow the editorial
line rather closely and the probability that they draw for individuals who
generally share their views on topical issues appear at worst immaterial
and at best assets in an examination of reader attitudes. That cartoons lack
balance and subtlety and are meant to awaken prejudices or aggressions in
the viewer may disqualify them in certain areas of historical writing; however, in an image study, this merely accentuates their importance. I fur-

ther believe that cartoons have very positive qualities that recommend them as evidence for an examination of public attitudes. For example, they often recall incidents that have been all but forgotten by historians but which at a given time could be used to arouse latent dislikes or fears. Also, repetition is the very essence of cartooning. For the cartoonists, no saying is too trite or too banal. Each has a mental storehouse of symbols that have gained credibility through use by successive generations of artists. Cartoonists not only draw upon that armory again and again; they manipulate symbols as though they were puppets which they cannot modify without destroying the meaning built around them. Consequently, cartoonists ordinarily are content to give an innovative twist to such classic symbols as Uncle Sam or John Q. Public and most often settle for something less. Hence, if a cartoon affords surprise it is a familiar surprise founded paradoxically enough on instant recognition. Cartoons thus provide invaluable clues to the mood and mores and underlying attitudes of the society that produced and accepted them. Finally, cartoons contribute highly visual nongovernmental variables to cross-cultural relations.

In a very real sense, the cartoonists themselves have dictated the emphasis of the chapters that follow. Their choice of symbols, their greater or lesser attention to Latin America in various time spans, and their interest or lack of interest in the individual republics and the kinds of domestic and international issues that attracted them were the basic considerations in the decisions I made with respect to which cartoons should be used. Within those broad areas I made judgmental decisions, including attempting to maintain a meaningful balance of topics. The problem of balance led me to underrepresent the cartoonists' representations of Latin America as a whole and their use of non-Black adult males. This resulted in females, children, Black adult males, and military-social issues being overrepresented. But the distortions were not in any sense of a degree to invalidate the overall conclusions that may be drawn about how and why cartoonists used the symbols they did in treating hemispheric affairs.

The distribution of cartoons according to time spans correlates quite closely with the attention that the artists gave to Latin America. Thus, during the decade and a half from 1897 to 1912—encompassing the war with Spain, the subsequent concerns over Cuba, the debates over canal treaties, and the fall of the highly regarded dictatorship of Porfirio Díaz in Mexico

—Latin America appeared regularly on the editorial pages. That is why a good share of the cartoons are from that era. Then, in the 1920s, Latin America again became the primary focus of our international relations. That time it was occasioned by our intervention in the Central American and Caribbean in efforts to establish political stability as a way of guaranteeing our national security interests and private investments, continuing difficulties with the "revolutionary" administrations in Mexico over subsoil rights and what was seen as President Plutarco Elías Calles' inclination toward international communism, and, finally, the growing distrust of the United States by the Latin American republics generally that by 1928 had surfaced at Havana and threatened to totally disrupt hemispheric relations. Latin America did not again capture the attention of the cartoonists until the early 1960s when initially they lined up nearly unanimously in support of the goals of the Alliance for Progress and in identifying the military and the economic elite as the obstacles to fulfilling these goals.

The distribution of the cartoons by regions also closely parallels the relative importance the cartoonists assigned them. An overwhelming majority of the cartoons deal with the Caribbean area, reflecting the United States' awareness of developments there. When the Caribbean region is broken down into its component parts, Cuba and Mexico share the limelight, with Costa Rica and El Salvador going nearly unnoticed. Until the 1960s and the coming of the Alliance for Progress and a new cycle of military governments, the interests of cartoonists in the republics south of Venezuela and Colombia were always marginal, except during World War II and the ideological conflicts related to it. The minimal concerns of cartoonists in the more southern republics speak eloquently to the larger point, namely that, historically, only under duress has the United States shown a strong and sustained interest in that part of Latin America not washed by the Caribbean.

It will be apparent to some readers that certain pervasive issues and pictorial devices are conspicuous by their paucity in the volume. Again, this is as the cartoonists would have it. There are few cartoons that even remotely reflect the profound antagonism felt before World War II by United States Protestants toward the Latin American varieties of Roman Catholicism. This is because historically the cartoonists have largely avoided that field, presumably because of respect for reader sensitivities or the possible economic consequences to publishers taking a pronounced anti-

28    Catholic stance. There are no cartoons that intentionally depict female figures unfavorably, because cartoonists have chosen not to employ feminine symbols for the purpose of communicating derogatory views of the peoples and institutions of the republics. Adult males with pronounced European features and Western dress appear sparingly because with few exceptions the artists have failed to credit Latin American males with playing roles commonly associated with responsible western European or Anglo-Saxon types. Social issues receive only limited attention in the volume because, throughout most of the period covered, cartoonists, much like the public for which they drew, failed to make the association between political instability and social inequities. Only with the appearance of the present generation of artists has this relationship begun to receive a share of the attention it deserves. Finally, the republics seldom appear dehumanized, because only occasionally have cartoonists gone to their animal zoos for symbolic representations of hemispheric issues.

If it seems, as it will to a large percentage of readers, that the cartoons included herein victimize the people of Latin America, it is because the cartoonists ordinarily have portrayed the republics as politically and economically impoverished and culturally deprived. Concomitantly, for the most part, they have been willing participants in a "grand design" to strip Latin Americans of any inherent ability to compete on equal terms in this hemisphere by denying them the very qualities required to compete in Western societies.

# 2. THE HEMISPHERE AS MONOLITH

The republics of Latin America have many features in common but also profound dissimilarities. They share a common experience of adaptation to a New World environment of open spaces and wide horizons. They share the marriage of two profoundly different cultures. They share complex religious beliefs. They share the experience of successfully struggling for independence from their Mother Countries. They share a common political philosophy, a common conception of human rights. Eighteen of the twenty republics share a common official language. Latin American scholars, especially in periods when they have felt their countries threatened, have tended to stress the sentiment of cultural solidarity. The search since World War II for success through myriad international agencies is a recent example of adversity at the national level prompting unity at the continental level.

But the notion of oneness ignores many of the realities of everyday life. Geography and climate have combined to fragment the continent into tropics, cold tablelands, temperate plains, and humid coastal belts, creating problems of communication and nurturing localism. Different indigenous peoples gave rise to distinct regional cultures that have persisted. Political independence did little to solve these differences, while intensifying the chauvinism of the new republics. In the twentieth century pragmatic politicians and concerned intellectuals turned chauvinism into an intense search for "individual" national character, such as *mexicanidad*, *argentinidad*, and *peruanidad*. The reoccurring urge to extend national boundaries led time and again to costly conflict and lasting enmities between Chileans and Bolivians, Peruvians and Ecuadorians, Brazilians and a half dozen of their neighbors, Haitians and Dominicans, Salvadorians and Hondurans—such a list could be extended easily.

Export economies oriented toward western Europe and the United States have tended until quite recently to discourage the development of commercial linkages of the kind that might have assisted the republics in overcoming their profound distrust of one another. Today, for a variety of reasons, the republics are in sharply contrasting stages of economic development, political modernization, social mobilization, and cultural maturity. Argentina and Honduras, for example, have taken radically different paths of development. The racial composition of the populations varies widely not only between but often within the respective republics. In the above context the growth of Pan American agencies and the Organization of American States is explained not by any strong sense of continentalism they hold but precisely because they give support to rather than threaten the concept of national sovereignty.

Historically, cartoonists have chosen to portray Latin America as a single entity or as composed of a number of states without regard for their strong dissimilarities. There are several possible explanations why this has been the case. First, the cartoonists risk the danger of diffusing attention from their argument if they pack their pictures with numerous figures, symbols, or labels. Second, based upon evidence drawn from the cartoons themselves, it seems clear that artists often have been woefully uninformed about the area and its issues, a situation that began to attenuate only after World War II. Third, the area is so complex and the reading public so unmindful of that complexity that there has been little point in artists' attempting to exploit uniqueness, even had they been so inclined. Fourth, the cartoonists have merely reflected the teachings of the standard scholarly literature of the past, which tended to stress commonness rather than differentiation. Fifth, the tendency is for units to converge when viewed from an extraneous angle. Sixth, in graphically presenting Latin America as a single unit, the artists, intentionally or otherwise, have simply opted to pay lip service to what Washington has said and not to what it has practiced in its relations with Latin America. Public officials who would be most unlikely openly to suggest a single policy for a region as diverse as western Europe repeatedly have created the impression that the United States has a single policy for the vast and varied Latin American area, based at different times on the Monroe Doctrine, the Big Stick, the Good Neighbor, or the Alliance for Progress, to mention only four of the better known "cornerstones." Actually, there has not yet been a time when a single United States policy could be applied simultaneously to, say, Mexico, Brazil, and Nicaragua; and Washington has never seriously pretended to be evenhanded in implementing such policies as recognition of new governments, fiscal and military intervention, military aid, hemispheric defense, or economic aid. Quite the contrary, the United States has insisted that its

broad hemispheric objectives be achieved, if achieved at all, through bilateral agreements and / or treaties. Thus, the cartoons appearing in this
chapter focus on the practice of artists not to differentiate between the
republics. The cartoons and the legends that accompany them are also
meant to suggest that the cartoonists' failure to individualize the republics
other than by labels has been one of the continuing reflections of the misunderstanding of hemispheric realities by United States Americans.

Following the Civil War, the United States quickly began to expand its commercial contacts with Europe, the Far East, and Middle America. Meanwhile, the fleet that had been assembled during the Civil War was permitted to rust away to the point where only two ships were considered serviceable. In trading circles, that situation was viewed as intolerable for a nation in competition with the imperial powers of Europe, and pressure for more up-to-date ships mounted. Finally, in 1883, Congress reluctantly appropriated funds for four new warships which became the nucleus of a modern steel navy.

When this cartoon by Thomas Nast, one of the United States' foremost editorial artists of all time, appeared in 1880, an "unprotected" Miss Columbia, at the time commonly employed to symbolize a righteous United States, was made to suffer insults from a cross-section of international rivals, including Mexico and Peru. As was the practice at the time and subsequently of often portraying the people of the various Latin American republics as indistinguishable one from another, the hair, complexion, headgear, clothing, cigars, and general demeanor of the Mexican and Peruvian figures are for all intents and purposes identical.

1.   **The Unprotected Female**
Thomas Nast, *Harper's Weekly*, February 21, 1880.

The Pan-American Exposition held at Buffalo in 1901 was sponsored to promote commercial and social interchange between the republics and the United States. In this cartoon, various Latin American peoples, identifiable only by their labels, lend support to a strident Uncle Sam, determined to defend the Monroe Doctrine against possible German territorial and commercial encroachments. The figure between Brazil and Mexico is labeled Patagonia. This raises the question: was the cartoonist unaware that Patagonia did not exist as a separate nation, was he using poetic license coupled with grand-scale ignorance, or did he possibly confuse Patagonia with Paraguay?

**2. The Great Balancing Act at Buffalo**
It takes the Yankee nation
To make equilibration.
But every time you turn around
Pop! goes the Kaiser!
(With apologies to the Weasel)
Albert Levering, *Harper's Weekly*, June 8, 1901.

By the Clayton-Bulwer Treaty concluded with Great
Britain in 1850, the United States agreed not to secure
exclusive control over the long-talked-about isthmian
canal. Thereafter, United States and British interests
in the construction of the canal languished until the
Spanish-American War when the dash of the battleship
*Oregon* from the Pacific coast around South America to
Cuban waters impressed upon Washington the advan-
tages of not only a canal but, furthermore, a canal under
the sole control of the United States. Great Britain, faced
with a hostile Europe and enmeshed in costly war in
South Africa, acceded in the Hay-Pauncefote Treaty
of 1901 to Washington's suggestion that the Clayton-
Bulwer Treaty be superseded by another which would
enable the United States to build and control an isthmian
canal unilaterally. Thus, Great Britain recognized United
States preeminence in the Western Hemisphere and in-
ferentially assigned to Uncle Sam the role of policeman
of the hemisphere, charged with protecting foreign interests from the caprices of governments in and around the
Caribbean.

In cartoonist Homer Davenport's version of the drama
of dividing up the globe, Latin America is stripped even of
a geographical identity. This calls attention to a pervasive
phenomenon in hemispheric affairs, namely that decisions profoundly affecting the people of Latin America
often have been made with little or no input from them
or regard for their reactions.

3. **Accepting the Monroe Doctrine**
John Bull gratefully admits that Uncle Sam is the proper custodian of the Western Hemisphere.
Homer Davenport, *Review of Reviews*, January 1902.

At the turn of the century the United States had a negative trade balance with Latin America. The First International Conference of American States (1889) and subsequent efforts to reverse the trend were ineffectual. Latin America continued to sell more to the United States than it bought. This cartoon reflects the importance that the United States attached to that condition. Cartoons of this genre, utilizing similar figures for a number of otherwise differentiated countries, played their part in perpetuating the stereotype of the Latin American republics as ungrateful neighbors.

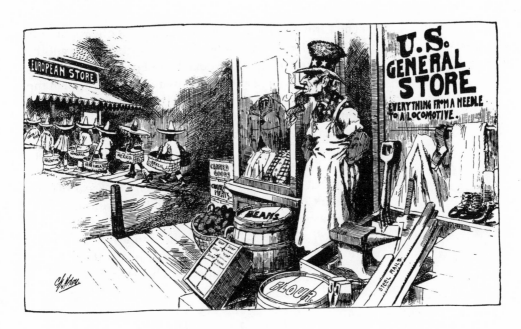

**4.** **Only His Neighbors Fail to Patronize Uncle Sam's Big Store**
*North American* (Philadelphia), 1902.

The Latin American republics early built one reputation in the United States for fiscal irresponsibility and another for carefree living. Debt defaults to European nations, especially by Venezuela, that invited intervention in the Caribbean were probably more disturbing to the United States than were the republics' failure to meet their obligations to United States creditors. What was considered the mismanagement of their monetary problems led first to the "Big Stick" policy of Theodore Roosevelt and later to official United States intervention in the fiscal affairs of certain Central American and Caribbean nations.

By portraying all of South America as "our southern brother," Charles L. "Bart" Bartholomew encapsulated the single-entity concept even more neatly than did those artists who relied upon labels to identify their subjects.

**5.** **Raising the Mortgage**

If our southern brother would raise more mortgage and less other things, no one would object.

Charles L. "Bart" Bartholomew, *Minneapolis Journal*, ca. 1903.

So far as the United States public was concerned, Germany constituted the greatest single threat to United States hegemony in the hemisphere during the early years of the century. Today scholars generally favor the view that Germany's ambitions and capabilities in the New World were exaggerated by groups in Washington interested in an isthmian canal, expanded trade with Latin America, and the creation of a sphere of influence worthy of a world power. Whatever the reason, any suggestion of German intrusion in the hemisphere was denounced as a potential violation of the Monroe Doctrine and that was more than enough to send the jingoists into action.

This cartoon was occasioned by suspicions that Germany was angling for a toehold in unstable Cuba and/or the Dutch West Indies and that in joining with Great Britain in the blockade of Venezuela—an enterprise which eventuated in the German bombardment of Venezuela's Fort San Carlos in January 1903—the Kaiser's motives went beyond simply collecting debts owed by Venezuela. In pursuing its anti-German policies, the United States did not need or solicit the support of the Latin American republics. This cartoonist chose to establish beyond any possible doubt the United States' ability to go it alone by portraying the republics as equally helpless and equally dependent.

6. **Five Battleships Ordered,—a Few More Supports for the Nest**
*Philadelphia Inquirer*, 1903.

One alternative to denigrating the republics by denying them individuality was to portray each of them as different from the others but so similar in size, dress, and general appearance as to invite ridicule if not contempt.

**7.   Room for All, If They're Careful**
William Allan Rogers, *New York Herald*, 1904.

An earlier cartoon (no. 6) depicted the republics as eggs in the "American" eagle's clutch. This caption, taken from the Mother Goose jingle, suggests that by the Third International Conference of American States (held in Rio de Janeiro in mid-1906) the republics at the conference could be lumped together arbitrarily since their appearances and voices were indistinguishable one from another. It is interesting to speculate whether the artist may also have had in mind the next line of the verse, "was not that a dainty dish to set before the king?" who metaphorically could only have been President Theodore Roosevelt. The cook is Elihu Root, secretary of state under Roosevelt and a proponent of strong leadership in Latin America along the lines of Porfirio Díaz in Mexico.

**8.    When the Pie was Open'd the Birds Began to Sing**
Garnett Warren, *Boston Herald*, 1906. Reprinted by permission: Boston Newspaper Division, The Hearst Corporation.

As noted above (see no. 6), Germany—here represented by the Kaiser—was held to offer serious economic competition to the United States in Latin America. In retrospect, it is apparent that the German threat was exaggerated at least in part in order to justify United States responses to it. In this instance, as in many other cartoons, Latin America is assigned a passive role, its fate left to be determined by outside forces.

### 9. The Oyster and the Shell

A condition Secretary Root is said to have faced in South America.
Charles L. "Bart" Bartholomew, *Minneapolis Journal*, 1906. Reprinted with permission of The Minneapolis Star and Tribune Company. All rights reserved.

This 1911 cartoon by Bartholomew appeared as the threat of war in Europe approached. At the time, the United States was stoutly opposed to this hemisphere's becoming entangled in European conflicts. Here Mother Hen Taft's frightened brood of Latin American republics hurries to the protection proffered by the United States. Bartholomew was but one of the many cartoonists who before World War I used the techniques of anonymity and dehumanization, thereby denying the Latin American republics a positive role in hemispheric affairs.

**10. The Real Peace Bird**

Charles L. "Bart" Bartholomew, *Minneapolis Journal*, 1911. Reprinted with permission of The Minneapolis Star and Tribune Company. All rights reserved.

The Pan American Union Building in Washington, D.C., houses the headquarters and many of the agencies of the Organization of American States as well as the Columbus Memorial Library. The original grant for the building came from Andrew Carnegie, industrialist and philanthropist. In May 1911, he contributed an additional one hundred thousand dollars toward completion of the structure.

The above cartoon, with President William Howard Taft in the background, records the recognition accorded to Mr. Carnegie by the American republics in appreciation of the material aid rendered by him "to the cause of peace and friendship between nations." The representations of the various Latin American nations, especially Mexico, still under Porfirio Díaz, whose prestige in the United States remained high, provide some suggestion of their individuality. The overall impression, however, is one of similarity rather than uniqueness.

**11. Benefactor of Humanity**
Mr. Carnegie being presented with a gold medal by the representatives of twenty-one American republics.
*Utica Saturday Globe*, 1911.

When this cartoon appeared in 1912, war clouds hovered over Europe, and the Panama Canal was but a few months away from completion. With those developments in mind, Uncle Sam asserts his claims to hegemony in the hemisphere under the terms of the Monroe Doctrine as unilaterally interpreted in Washington. The artist apparently was in full accord with those in government who would deny the republics a participatory role in policies vitally affecting their well-being and sovereignty.

12. **His Hat (Monroe Doctrine) Is in the Ring**
    Charles L. "Bart" Bartholomew [?], *Minneapolis Journal*, 1912. Reprinted with
    permission of the *St. Paul Dispatch*.

On April 21, 1914, United States marines occupied the
port of Veracruz, Mexico, with the stated objective of
fulfilling President Woodrow Wilson's announced determination to topple Victoriano Huerta, the military dictator who had seized the presidency of Mexico following
the assassination of President Francisco Madero. Huerta
refused to buckle under and received support from his
political opposition. Wilson, as a consequence, found
himself faced with an "unthinkable" Mexican war. The
ABC powers (Argentina, Brazil, and Chile) opportunely
stepped in with an offer of mediation, which Wilson
hastily accepted, as a means of deliverance from a humiliating predicament. ABC delegates and representatives
of the United States and Mexico met at Niagara Falls,
Canada, in late May and agreed upon a plan which en-
abled the United States to avoid war. The ABC powers'
offer of mediation and their subsequent statesmanship
at the Niagara Conference, which took place against a
backdrop of war in Europe, provided cartoonists with
one of the few occasions in over one hundred years that
they have taken to portray the republics in a favorable
light. The use, however, of a single figure to represent
all of Latin America, except Mexico, implied a cultural
unity and agreement on hemispheric policy that has
never existed except in the minds of some non–Latin
Americans.

**13. United We Stand**

North and South America getting together on the Mexican situation.

Charles L. "Bart" Bartholomew, *St. Paul Daily News*, 1915. Reprinted with the permission of the *St. Paul Dispatch*.

In early 1916, when this cartoon appeared in the *Review
of Reviews*, war raged in Europe, and in North America
relations with Mexico were tense. Within months the
prospects of direct United States involvement in Europe
had increased, and nearer home John J. Pershing had
been named to lead a punitive expedition into Mexico in
pursuit of the revolutionary Pancho Villa. There was
good reason for the United States to take advantage of
improved relations with the republics resulting from
President Wilson's pledge that the United States never
again would seek additional territory in Latin America by
conquest, his acceptance of the ABC powers' offer of
mediation in the controversy arising over United States
occupation of Veracruz, and his early withdrawal of
troops from the occupied port to make a show of Western Hemisphere unity. The figure labeled "South America" (read Latin America) is shown in an unusual role for
a Latin American male personality, that of appearing in
Western-style dress and in stature and demeanor the
equal of the United States representative, in this case
President Wilson.

**14.  EUROPE: "If I had only done that!"**
Westerman[?], *Ohio State Journal* (Columbus), 1916. Reprinted by permission of
the *Columbus Citizen-Journal*.

During 1923 the Central American republics agreed to a number of pacts, a key objective of which was that the five republics would not recognize governments that should come to power through a coup d'état or revolution. Before the pacts could be ratified, a defeated presidential candidate in Honduras resorted to revolution. The United States declared its intention to implement the policy of the new pacts. It broke off formal relations, sent warships to both coasts, and landed marines. Washington, in cooperation with Nicaragua, Guatemala, Costa Rica, and El Salvador, selected and recognized a provisional government. At home, continued United States involvement in Honduras raised the question: was Washington primarily concerned with the manner in which Hondurans settled their election disputes or was the main objective of intervention the protection of United States capital already invested in Honduras, especially when rumors of important oil strikes in that country were in circulation? One of the cartoonists' favorite devices has been to portray the Latin American republics as parts of Uncle Sam's anatomy. And when he has felt pain in his neck, chest, shoulders, or lower regions, he has ordinarily prescribed for himself a self-administered "dose of Monroe Doctrine."

**15. Another Little Touch of Sore Throat**
Paul Plaschke, *Louisville Times*, 1924. Reprinted by permission of the *Louisville Times*.

The artist on this occasion apparently was engaging in wishful thinking as a result of the favorable receptions that Charles A. Lindbergh received during his good will tour to several of the republics following his conquest of the Atlantic in the *Spirit of St. Louis*. At no time during the tour did a responsible United States representative publicly propose that Latin America be welcomed even as a partner in respect to the Monroe Doctrine and its interpretation. Furthermore, any expectations for improved relations generated by Lindbergh's barnstorming had dissipated within weeks, and at the Havana Conference hemispheric relations reached what up to then was an all-time low.

**16.  The Monroe Doctrine Now Seems to Have a Little Brother**
John T. McCutcheon, *Chicago Tribune*, ca. 1928. Reprinted, courtesy of the *Chicago Tribune*.

Cartoonists and editors offered various interpretations of the successes and failures of the Sixth International Conference of American States that met in Havana in January 1928. But former Secretary of State Charles Evans Hughes, head of the United States delegation, was generally acclaimed for having headed off possible disruption of relations on several occasions. This cartoon refers to the near breakup of the conference over a resolution that "no state has the right to intervene in the internal affairs of another." The breakup was averted and a final vote on the resolution headed off when Hughes "in a supreme effort" defended the right of "interposition of a temporary character." The United States thus preserved the right of direct intervention. That right was renounced within five years and the renunciation was respected in principle until the United States landed troops in the Dominican Republic in 1965. In this cartoon, naturally, only five of the twenty republics constitute the Pan American Union basketball team, and there is no way to identify by nationality any one of them. Collectively, neither these five nor possible substitutes had any chance against the United States one-man opposition.

**17.** **Guarding the Basket**

J. N. "Ding" Darling, *New York Herald Tribune*, 1928. Copyright, 1928, Des Moines
Register and Tribune Company. Reprinted by permission.

Among the favorite themes of the cartoonists has been one that portrayed the republics as unwilling or incapable of contributing responsibly to their own welfare and development. This drawing appeared when the era of the Good Neighbor Policy had ended and Washington's financial assistance to Latin America was minimal. Aside from stereotypically ascribing to the republics a preference for handouts over hard work and saving, the device of using a single figure to symbolize Latin America served to obscure the fact that the United States hemispheric policies, most especially those in the economic sphere, traditionally have been designed to treat the republics on a bilateral basis.

**18. A Little More Effort, Señor**
Hugh Hutton, *Philadelphia Inquirer*, 1961. Reprinted by permission of *The Philadelphia Inquirer*.

As a century of cartooning certifies, the United States
has held that through pressure from Washington the
Latin American republics would ultimately adopt United
States–style democracy. President John F. Kennedy was
convinced that political freedom could destroy the traditional social barriers. At his insistence the declaration
that political freedom must accompany material progress
was made an integral part of the Alliance for Progress.
There was an abundance of evidence by 1963 that, so
far as democracy was concerned, leaders in many of the
republics were less than apt learners. Here a pedantic
Uncle Sam is thwarted by a uniformly contrary Latin
American class. By portraying the political situation in
the various republics in undifferentiated terms, this artist
reinforced the historically inaccurate view of a "monolith" to the south of the United States.

**19. The Class Will Please Come to Order—Somebody?**
William H. Crawford, *New York Times*, December 22, 1963. Reprinted by permission of Newspaper Enterprise Association.

This 1962 drawing by Bill Mauldin is one of the most artistically impressive and meaningful cartoons ever to appear on Latin America. The Alliance for Progress was only a few months old, but already there was abundant evidence that it was on its way to failure in a number of areas, including that of reform. The impact of the cartoon derives principally from the brilliant exploitation of the stereotypical image of the "lazing Latin" about to suffer the consequences of his insincere commitment to meaningful reform.

**20.** Bill Mauldin. © 1962. Reprinted by permission of Bill Mauldin.

# 3. LATIN AMERICA AS FEMALE

At various times in the past, our cartoonists have chosen to portray the Latin American republics as feminine. The occasions of female symbolization and the roles in which female characters have been cast have owed nothing to happenstance. Even allowing for specific differences in interpretation, the general messages that the artists wanted transmitted to their public seem no less clear. It is apparent that certain deep-seated and continuing convictions about role differentiation by sex in the United States have been reflected in such cartoons. A cursory review of the multiple roles that cartoonists have tended to emphasize in their depictions of Latin America supports this claim.

Of the various schools of thought about women in United States society since the Civil War, two dichotomize their status in ways that are particularly relevant to this study. The first emphasizes the changing status of women, changes that are closely linked to new situations arising out of an environment increasingly dominated by industrialization and urbanization. It points to women's ever-heightening intellectual standing; the rights won to hold title to property and to establish businesses; their access to courts, enfranchisement, and new economic opportunities outside the home; and concomitantly their greater capacity to restrain parental and husbandly authority and greater freedom in manners and morals. Those who favor this approach recognize that there are still numerous battles to be fought and victories to be won but nonetheless believe that the lines between male and female spheres, whether intellectual, economic, or social, have blurred.[1] In directing attention to the Western Hemisphere by the use of female symbols, the cartoonists have chosen to disregard those new female roles associated with the late nineteenth and twentieth centuries, preferring instead to depict their Latin American females as dependents, or sex symbols, or simply objects to elicit sympathy, roles associated especially with the early and mid-nineteenth century.

The second school stresses what it sees as the striking continuity of beliefs and attributes about women held by succeeding generations of men. It contends that the dominant influences upon female lifestyles in the United States have been those traditionally associated with the patriarchal society. Nineteenth-century theological assumptions about the

weakness and inferiority of women and nativist concerns about the wife
and mother in the midst of the rapid industrialization and the wave of immigration around 1900 have been complemented in this century by the
pervasiveness of Freudian analysis, which depicts females as passive creatures in contrast to active males. The forces at work, the argument continues, reaffirm woman's alleged dependence upon man for food, shelter,
and clothing. She is powerless in her own right. Her destiny becomes marriage, for which she prepares by cultivating seductiveness, gentility, and
submissiveness. She is Keats's "milkwhite lamb that bleats for man's protection." In the view of feminist Charlotte Perkins Gilman, sex in effect
becomes her economic way of life and hence marriage becomes legalized
prostitution. In recognition of her passive virtues, her menfolk have assigned her, as Mother, an official position alongside God and home in the
sentimental triad of proclaimed American values. If she be maintained in
luxury she plays the added role of status symbol, establishing that her hus-
band competes successfully in a system that places paramount importance on material achievement. In recognition of her purity, the nation,
meanwhile, has made her the symbol of peace and justice and the magnan-
imous goddess of liberty in contrast to the shrewd, grasping, horsetrading
Uncle Sam. Cartoonists have depended almost entirely upon this set of
traditional images in their representation of Latin America as feminine.

As female, then, Latin America has been White and privileged, as have
been women about whom image makers in the United States have been
basically concerned. The cartoon characters have played the three basic
ascriptive roles assigned to women in the traditional division of labor.
Sometimes they are attractive, seductive types seemingly anxious to yield
to superior males in return for support. Sometimes they are virtuous but
defenseless creatures requiring the protection of chivalrous or indulgent
males from the exploitation of undesirable European suitors. Sometimes
they have been physically fragile individuals inviting the sympathy and
understanding of benevolent neighbors. In sum, Latin America caricatured as female has been weak, dependent, inadequate, in very crucial
ways. Nations and peoples so depicted have been denied characteristics
which might have qualified them as equal partners in the hemisphere.
The feminine representations of Latin America, in fact, seem to lend credence to the dictum that only in the human race has the thought occurred
that one sex should be dependent entirely on the other.

The United States, under President Wilson's and Secretary of State William Jennings Bryan's leadership, is shown capitulating to what the cartoonist considered unreasonable demands on the United States by Great Britain over developments in Mexico while failing to protect United States citizens, witnessed by the list in Uncle Sam's back pocket. This behavior is portrayed as womanly and unbecoming. Although Uncle Sam is addressed as "sir," he is in high heels and ruffled pants, his hair in ringlets. The cartoon calls attention to some of the very basic assumptions about males and females that have prevailed in the United States and have been used by cartoonists to establish ordinate and subordinate roles in hemisphere affairs.

**21. Suppose Mexico Should Harm Another Subject of Great Britain?**
Reynolds, *Oregonian* (Portland), 1914.

Prior to 1920, cartoonists commonly portrayed Latin American states as female when seeking to invoke compassion for them. Here defenseless Mexico is cast as a woman—with stereotypical American Indian features—and Catholic (note wall hangings), threatened by Great Britain (*center*), Spain (*left*), and France (*right*), who in late 1861 sent expeditionary forces to Mexico with the stated intention of enforcing the financial claims of their subjects. Public sympathy in the United States was on the side of Mexico, but the Civil War erased for the moment any possibility that Washington, in the name of the Monroe Doctrine, might resist the invaders. Great Britain and Spain withdrew when satisfied that Mexico under Benito Juárez was committed to fulfilling its obligations to the extent that internal conditions permitted. France's ambitious Napoleon III, however, determined to remain and to establish a New World empire. Mexican patriots resisted and the project collapsed in 1867 before the United States became directly involved.

**22. The Sick Woman of Mexico**

JOHN BULL: "Say, Missus! me and these other Gents 'ave come to Nurse you a bit."
Frank Bellew, *Harper's Weekly*, February 8, 1862.

United States agricultural and industrial output spurted following the Civil War, calling forth vigorous efforts to open overseas markets capable of absorbing the mounting surpluses. Latin America, where commercial relations earlier had been left to develop haphazardly, became a prime focus of attention for traders and public officials working in behalf of the private sector.

This cartoon, which called attention to the New Orleans–sponsored "World's International Cotton Centennial Exposition" of 1884–85 and which meant to create a positive image of Latin America as a trading partner, is an early example of what became standard practice among cartoonists of using European-like females to present the republics favorably. The dark-hued figure in non-European attire and labeled La Plata (read Argentina) is interesting because by 1884 the Argentine population, along with that of Uruguay, was the most European in all of Latin America and probably in the entire Western Hemisphere.

**23.** Now Peace hath done her perfect work—serene,
Loyal and beautiful, the Southern queen
Bids all the wide world welcome to her door,
Where Industry has spread a varied store,
Where the white splendor of her heaping bales
Answers the snow of crowding foreign sails—
Wise sister, blessed be thy welcoming hand,
Stretched to Republics of the tropic land!
Joseph Keppler, *Puck*, December 10, 1884.

This cartoon, appearing two years before the Spanish-American War erupted, contains all the elements of a melodrama, a highly popular art form of the era. Textbooks, journals, and newspapers had prepared the United States public to view Spain as a villain against humanity in general and against the welfare of Cuba in particular. By the same token, Uncle Sam, backed by a modernizing navy, had become the self-appointed, daring, chivalrous defender of the hemisphere. So long as the cartoonists favored Cuba's cause, it was ordinarily physiognomized as female and Caucasian.

## 24. The Cuban Melodrama

THE NOBLE HERO (*to the* HEAVY VILLAIN): "Stand back, there, gol darn ye!—If you force this thing to a fifth act, remember that's where I git in *my* work!"
C. Jay Taylor, *Puck*, June 3, 1896.

This cartoon appeared soon after the political cartoon became a regular feature of the mass media and at a time when United States interest in Cuba was intensifying. It had been generally agreed that Spain's days in Cuba were numbered and that the United States would not permit events on the island to run their course unattended. There remained, however, considerable difference of opinion on how United States interests might best be advanced. One popular choice was to free Cuba from Spain and annex it as the forty-sixth state in the Union. In his suggestion of a romance in which Cuba plays the subordinate role of a señorita eagerly responding to Uncle Sam's advances, the artist created a scenario that his successors have reproduced with timely variations when seeking to mobilize support for the improvement of relations between the United States and Latin America.

**25. Come Live with Me and Be My Love!**
(Uncle Sam is wooing Cuba, while jealous Spain is plotting revenge in the shadow)
F. T. Richards[?], *Life* (New York), 1896.

This widely reproduced cartoon appeared at a time when demands for Spain's expulsion from the hemisphere had reached fever pitch in the United States. It associates Spanish tyranny with the sixteenth-century conquistadors Cortés and Pizarro as well as General "Butcher" Weyler of "reconcentration" camp fame in Cuba. The emaciated, prostrate female symbolizing Cuban misery was meant to enlist sympathy for the colony where Spain's reported atrocities fed the standard view of its assumed historical inhumanities.

**26. Spain's "Sense of Justice"**
C. G. Bush, *New York World*, 1898.

On April 25, 1898, President William McKinley approved an act of Congress which declared that the United States was at war with Spain as of April 21. Anticipating Cuba's freedom from Spain, this cartoonist drew a slender, bony-armed female with Caucasian features enshrouded in the Cuban flag and arising from the shackles of colonialism. Thus, his public was invited simultaneously to share Cuba's emancipation and to commiserate with the former colony as it faced the uncertainties of the future.

**27. Cuba Libre!**
William Allan Rogers, *Harper's Weekly*, April 30, 1898.

Following the outcome of the Spanish-American War,
influential elements in the United States were sharply
divided as to whether the island should be given its sovereignty or be annexed to the United States. The issue
ultimately was compromised by making Cuba a quasi
protectorate of the United States under the Platt Amendment. Those in favor of annexation had to confront the
view of their opponents that the Cuban people were
basically Black and anarchic and as such unqualified to
practice political democracy. This cartoon reflects the
annexationists' tactical responses to the Black-anarchic
contention: make Cuba "fair" to qualify it for democracy
and female to evoke not only the image of peace and
order but also the need to be protected. A benevolent
United States in turn is symbolized as female.

**28. Miss Cuba Receives an Invitation**
MISS COLUMBIA (*to her fair neighbor*): "Won't you join the stars and be my forty-sixth?"
*Chicago Record-Herald*, 1901.

The annexationists defeated, Uncle Sam prepared to leave the island to a fair maiden, cast in the familiar role of housecleaning, about to apply her broom to Cuban politics. Some United States cartoonists (see chapters 4 and 5) and many informed Cubans, with good reason as it turned out, were dubious both of Cuba's ability to assume the responsibilities of sovereignty and of the United States' intention to allow it a serious attempt to do so.

**29. Packing Up**
*New York Tribune*, 1902.

Many individuals who followed developments in the Caribbean worried that Cuba's chances of survival as a new nation were being jeopardized by excessively severe tariffs levied by the United States on Cuban sugar and tobacco. In this cartoon, the figures representing Congress and the sugar trusts are the villains. If Cuba is revived, it is made to appear that it will have all the necessary ethnic and passive qualities to be acceptable to the United States. In the meantime, right-minded individuals could take pity on Cuba, victimized by greedy monopolists.

**30. Abandoned**
F. I. Richards, *New York Herald*, 1902.

Independent Cuba soon ran into economic straits. Elements in the United States who felt that Washington had a moral obligation to assist Cuba and those who believed that trade promised the surest way of maintaining effective control of the Cuban people supported proposals to grant Cuban sugar and tobacco special tariff concessions. This position was countered by the beet sugar and tobacco interests, whose lobbyists were influential in preventing the passage of legislation that the lower-tariff advocates considered reasonable and just. This cartoon—one of several that appeared in favor of generous reciprocity agreements—put added weight behind the case by presenting Miss Cuba as unassuming and possessing virtues that were much a part of the United States ethnic: cleanliness, self-reliance, enterprise, and thrift (note handbag).

**31.  I Come to Buy, Not to Beg, Sir**
William Allan Rogers, *Harper's Weekly*, November 7, 1903.

Growing international trade and the Spanish-American War in which the United States Navy was called upon to fight in two oceans heightened demands for an isthmian canal. When the second Hay-Pauncefote Treaty of 1901 with Great Britain gave the United States a free hand to build, control, and fortify a canal, it only remained for Washington to choose between the proposed Nicaraguan and Panamanian routes. Each route had had its champions for several years, but by late 1901 congressional and expert opinion had veered sharply toward Nicaragua, largely on the basis of costs. At that point the French-controlled New Panama Canal Company panicked. As heir to the de Lesseps group that had foundered in a sea of debt while attempting to construct a canal across the isthmus, the New Panama Canal Company, fearful of losing out entirely, slashed the asking price for its rights across Panama by 60 percent. The artist saw that gesture as the occasion for a "fickle" Uncle Sam to reject a consenting Miss Nicaragua and direct his attention to Miss Panama, obviously ready and willing to yield to Uncle Sam.

**32.** **MISS NICARAGUA:** "O Sam, you fickle thing! They tell awful stories about her!"
*Columbus* (Ohio) *Dispatch*, ca. 1902.

Porfirio Díaz, whose long dictatorial and socially backward regime was seen in many quarters as giving Mexico
much needed order and fiscal responsibility, had a generally friendly press in the United States. Complimentary
reference to him continued to appear in newspapers and
periodicals after the defeat of his armies by the rebel
forces of Francisco Madero. Here Díaz is depicted as
renouncing the presidency to a female Mexico whose
physical features and general attractiveness make her a
reasonable candidate for the favorable attention of Uncle
Sam, whom the cartoonists often portrayed as susceptible to the charms of unthreatening females.

**33.  Díaz Making His Greatest Gift to His Country**
(Referring to his renunciation of the presidency)
William Allan Rogers, *New York Herald*, 1911.

Nothing has been more effective in making the United States public receptive to favorable views of Latin America than those conflicts and ideologies born in Europe which have threatened to spill over into the hemisphere and thus to pose security concerns for the United States. This cartoon plays upon that fundamental fact but does not note that strained relations with the newly recognized, strongly nationalist government of Venustiano Carranza in Mexico was an added inducement for the United States to seek better understanding between the remaining republics of the hemisphere. When the cartoon appeared in the February 1916 issue of the *Review of Reviews*, President Wilson had only recently terminated the military occupation of Veracruz, leaving behind an atmosphere of bitterness. During the month following the cartoon's publication, the Mexican rebel leader Pancho Villa and his band raided across the border, taking the lives of seventeen United States citizens. That act prompted the fruitless Pershing expedition which contributed to the further deterioration of trust between the two nations. The artist, then, as a consequence of developments abroad and at home, had good reason to favor hemispheric unity but not, obviously, at the price of recommending a reordering of associations on a man-to-man basis.

**34.  Room for All under the New Umbrella**
Charles L. "Bart" Bartholomew, *Minneapolis News*, ca. 1916. Reprinted with permission of The Minneapolis Star and Tribune Company. All rights reserved.

The Fifth International Conference of American States met in Santiago, Chile, during March, April, and May of 1923 in an atmosphere of widespread suspicion over the motives and purposes of the United States. Mexico had refused to attend the conference because Washington had denied recognition to the Alvaro Obregón government. At a more general level, the republics were uniformly resentful over the steadfast determination of the United States to interpret unilaterally the Monroe Doctrine. The artist here suggests a brighter side to a gloomy situation. Presumably as a result of their participation in the war, the peace conference, and the deliberations of the League of Nations, the republics were seen as growing up and already had attained sufficient feminine maturity and charm once again to arouse Uncle Sam's amorous instincts.

**35. My, How You Have Grown!**

Sykes, *Philadelphia Evening Public Ledger*, 1923. Reprinted by permission of *The Philadelphia Inquirer*, 1923.

The sky pilot in this cartoon is Charles A. Lindbergh. Following his solo flight across the Atlantic in May 1927 and his return to a hero's welcome, he was enjoined by the United States government in December to make a good will flight to Mexico. When his reception in Mexico exceeded all expectations, his visit was extended to the Central American states, Colombia, Venezuela, Haiti, and Cuba, in all of which he was warmly received. Many cartoonists, reflecting editorial comment, predicted permanent gains from Colonel Lindbergh's mission. The artist on this occasion went a step beyond the usual love affair theme reserved for such occasions, to unite the United States and Mexico in wedlock.

**36. The Sky Pilot Performs a Wedding**
Cargill, *South Bend Tribune*, 1928. Reprinted by permission of the *South Bend Tribune*.

In January 1928, less than a month after Lindbergh's triumphal tour, the Sixth International Conference of American States met at Havana, Cuba. At the same time, United States marines were in Nicaragua and United States financial advisers were stationed throughout the Caribbean. Latin American feelings toward the United States had never been more bitter. The republics' deep concern over United States conduct did not prevent this cartoonist from hoping that an engaging and protective Uncle Sam could turn the thoughts of a worried señorita to lighter matters.

**37.** UNCLE SAM: "It's the wind, rustling the palms."
Jerry Doyle, *Philadelphia Record*, 1927. Reprinted by permission of Jerry Doyle.

Following the Havana Conference and United States insistence upon the right of "interposition of a temporary character," in December 1928 President-elect Herbert Hoover took a seven-week good will tour to more than half of the nations to the south in an effort to turn the tide of resentment and to present the "real Uncle Sam." The junket temporarily generated good will in some quarters, although numerous knowledgeable individuals failed to share the view of the figure here symbolizing Latin America. Instead, figuratively speaking, recalling the not-unusual consequences of whirlwind affairs for unwary, wide-eyed females, they remained deeply apprehensive of United States intentions, which at best ordinarily placed them in a decidedly subordinate role.

**38. Not as Bad as Painted**
Thiele, *Culver* (Ind.) *Citizen*, 1928. Reprinted by permission of the *Citizen*.

The favorable influences of the Good Neighbor Policy
and the hemispheric cooperation prompted by World
War II had largely dissipated when Dwight D. Eisenhower assumed the presidency. Throughout his term of
office, Europe and Asia commanded Washington's sustained attention to the near-total official neglect of hemisphere issues. Here the artist suggests the Eisenhower-
Dulles approach as one detrimental to Latin America
and calls attention to a new danger—the Russian bear—
in the Western Hemisphere. The artist, as had many of
his predecessors, relies upon the traditional strong-male/
weak-female roles of the leading characters in order to
convey his view of the proper conduct of hemisphere
affairs.

**39. Bypassed**
Rogerson, *Newsday*, 1954. Reprinted by permission of *Newsday*.

Soon after his inauguration, President Kennedy launched the Alliance for Progress, designed simultaneously to counter the influence of the USSR and Castro's Cuba and to help Latin America help itself. Congress appropriated initial funds in May 1961, a charter was agreed to in August, and President and Mrs. Kennedy toured Venezuela and Colombia in December to add emphasis to the New Frontier's concern for Latin America's welfare. This cartoon appeared when interest in and hopes for the Alliance were peaking. The euphoria of the time called for the use of a female figure to symbolize Latin America. When disillusionment set in, as it did within months, cartoonists reverted, as they traditionally had, to the use of male figures to represent the republics.

**40. We're Getting Better Gradually—Only Our Parrot Looks Bad**
*New York Times*, December 31, 1961. © 1961 by The New York Times Company.
Reprinted by permission.

The Alliance for Progress had barely been launched when skeptics in Latin America and the United States questioned the validity of its basic tenet: the idea that capital and further incorporation into world trade would solve all problems. For the doubters, large United States public investments in the republics only bought time against expropriation of foreign-owned properties, promoted United States exports, and reinforced direct intervention by Washington in the internal affairs of the republics. It was, furthermore, humiliating for the recipients to comply with conditions attached to "aid funds." In the economic area, those who were unenthusiastic about the Alliance contended that what was needed was price stabilization, improved terms of trade, and, as this cartoon suggests, "trade, not aid." The cartoon appeared about the time that the women's liberation movement began to gather momentum. Whether or not the movement has restrained cartoonists from relying upon the male-female theme, with all that the relationship has traditionally implied, remains to be seen, but the indications are that it has had that effect.

**41. I'd Rather Have Them Drink More Coffee**
Ed Valtman, *Hartford Times*, 1963. Reprinted by permission of Ed Valtman.

# 4. THE REPUBLICS AS CHILDREN

Following the Spanish-American War, cartoonists commonly made use of infant-youth and child-adult symbolism in pictorializing hemispheric issues. Mexico, the Caribbean nations, and the Central American republics were, as a consequence, repeatedly represented as infants or youths to call attention to their immaturity, while the United States was assigned parental and/or guardian roles. The artists scrapped these particular kinds of characterizations about the time of the Great Depression. The phenomenon itself, its discard, and its significance for the better understanding of hemispheric relations are understandable strictly in terms of domestic developments and attitudes.

The generation during which the youth and youth-adult analogies were exploited paralleled those early years of intense public interest in the child and child rearing in the United States. Before, during, and after World War I, parents, nurture writers, educators, religious figures, and public officials, under the influence of the developing sciences, especially psychology, debated endlessly the impact of industrial growth and urbanization, the entrepreneurial system, and immigration upon the child and the child-centered family. Adults were at counterpoint as to whether children should be considered diminutive men and women or innocent individuals who because of their tender years and inexperience must be protected from the worst influences of the environmental changes the United States was undergoing. The God-fearing and those who trusted nature debated the questions. Are children, as the Calvinists had insisted, born depraved and demonic in nature or are they God's little people with the potential for responsible self-fulfillment in adulthood? Would they comprise a better society or were they sons and daughters who would grow up and have thoughts similar to those of their parents? Such questions inevitably led to others. Should discipline be sufficiently painful to break the child's will or should it be limited to deprivation and appeals to the child's rationality? Who should be held responsible and to what degree when a child failed to fulfill achievement norms—child, parent, school, or society?

When the era opened, the individual dominated production and marketing; by its close, bureaucratically controlled industry was fast supplant-

ing family-owned enterprise. The competing systems threatened to produce irreconcilable objectives, and the child often became the victim of
disagreements about how best to serve the needs of a society in transition.
The entrepreneurially oriented elements, who tended toward activity instead of toward an accommodative style of behavior, basically favored
routinized child rearing as a way of inculcating problem solving and self-
control. Youngsters, they thought, should be taught to curb their immediate desires in the interest of satisfying long-range needs. The success ethic,
a cornerstone of their thinking, made idleness and shiftlessness unpardon-
able sins but Huckleberry Finn's natural boisterousness, self-sufficiency,
and resourcefulness admirable. Achievement was its own reward.

The newly emerging bureaucratic sectors, meanwhile, held a quite
different set of values and attitudes. They tended to reject routinized
training in favor of permissiveness, which they trusted gave children more
freedom for self-determination and would help them to develop a manipu-
lative stance toward their environment. They countered the persisting
view that life is an investment for which the reward would be reaped only
in the future with a consumption-oriented concept that accentuated immediate gratification. It followed that achievement might reasonably be
supplemented by directly rewarding experiences. Permissiveness and
immediate consumption combined to produce a "fun morality" that challenged traditional parental and educational philosophies about work and
play.

The uncertainties about child rearing, great as they were, did not prevent those concerned about youths from reaching consensus in two areas
particularly relevant to our subject. They agreed that female children
started off with virtues lacking in male children and that girls, consequently, were more obedient and cooperative and quicker to develop
those skills, traits, and value attitudes associated with the performance of
present and anticipated social roles. And the disputants realized that,
while there was a genetic relationship of childhood to the future, society
had not evolved any clearly demarcated step or rites by which youth could
advance to adulthood.

Conflicting opinions about children and adult responsibilities to
them provided the cartoonists with a wide range of currently interesting
areas from which to draw when they opted to cast hemisphere issues in
childlike symbols. And they took full advantage of their opportunities.

Sometimes they reflected views held over from an earlier age or from their own childhoods when corporal punishment and humiliations were favored methods of child control. At other times they applied up-to-date attitudes about children and child rearing to international situations, as when they advocated patience and understanding or rewarding of minor achievements. On still other occasions they went beyond the spectrum of commonly debated views, as when they suggested that the lowly regarded Blacks, Indians, and Spanish Catholics might produce offspring capable of evolving responsible political systems within a single generation, thereby seemingly favoring an environmentalist over a hereditary interpretation as a factor in human development. Always they operated on the widely accepted principle that girls have virtues that boys do not possess.

But whether drawing upon the past or the present attitudes toward children and their relationship to adults, the cartoonists' young people were almost invariably abnormal. Their "approved" boys and girls were too neat, too proper, too docile, and at their best when pleasing adults by displaying unrealistic appreciation of what the artist considered responsible behavior. On the other hand, their "disapproved" young people were dishevelled, unruly, quarrelsome, unteachable, impulsive dark-skinned males, determined not to learn the art of self-control. From the "approved—disapproved" dichotomy one must conclude that at the very least the approved had learned how to ingratiate themselves with those adults who took more satisfaction in children being dutiful and having adult interests than in seeing them develop their own unique personalities, and that the disapproved were set on playing undesirable, nuisance roles whatever the costs.

However inappropriate the analogy may have been when applied to sovereign states, portraying nationals as children was a more favorable characterization than representing them as adult females. A child figure at least carried within itself the presumed genetic capacity to grow up without predetermined limitations on the abilities of the eventual adult. On the other hand, as observed in chapter 3, being represented as an adult female strongly suggested that although a nation had reached maturity it could play only a quite limited number of roles and those of a nature that in the United States was considered to require a dominant male partner for successful fulfillment. But if child symbolism was fairer in a relative sense to the recipient, it still helped to perpetuate at Latin America's expense

the tendency in our culture to regard every situation as having a domi-
nance-submission relationship.

Equally to the point, the news media did not permit the public to focus on any hemisphere issue long enough for biological changes to be evidenced, even if some cartoonists at some time might have entertained that possibility. The consequences were that cartoon children never grew up to where they might reasonably be expected to strike out on their own and the reading public was encouraged to think of Latin America as a child-dependent suspended in time.

There is no hard evidence which explains satisfactorily why the cartoonists ceased to portray the Latin American nations as children after 1930. However, four possible factors suggest themselves. First, while child care remained a central concern after 1930, its novelty had worn thin. Second, the newest republics of Latin America—Cuba and Panama— were by the onset of the Great Depression a full generation old. But in that regard it should be appreciated that throughout the period cartoonists had taken the liberty of greatly prolonging Mexico's and the Central American republics' infancy, since Mexico dated its independence from 1810 and the Central American states from the 1820s. Third, there was a growing sensitivity to the implications of social relationships and, hence, of the inequalities explicit in treating some nations as children and others as adults. Fourth, abandoning the use of child symbolism in dealing with inter-American relations coincided with the beginning of the Good Neighbor Policy, a major proposed objective of which was to stress equality among the republics of the hemisphere. Representing Latin America as childlike and the United States as a mature guardian or protector was grossly inconsistent with that goal.

By the close of 1898, Hawaii had been annexed and Spain had relinquished its sovereignty over Cuba and had ceded the Philippines, Puerto Rico, and Guam outright to the United States. The acquisitions launched this country as a full-scale imperial power in competition with Great Britain and Germany. Cartoonists commonly used infant and childlike figures to express their views for and against imperialism and, once debate on that issue subsided, to express their convictions on matters that arose from United States imperial ventures. Mischievous infants were used in this cartoon to recall two points repeatedly raised by the anti-imperialists: (*a*) empire would create more problems than it was worth, and (*b*) the political maturity of the new members of the imperial family was such that they must in effect be denied full rights under the constitution.

**42. How Some Apprehensive People Picture Uncle Sam after the War**
*Detroit News*, 1898.

For a decade after the defeat of Spain, trade relations with Cuba and its political and economic instability were high on the United States foreign relations agenda. Controversy in the United States over tariffs on Cuban sugar and tobacco provided the occasion for this cartoon. During this period of intense concern, infants and children symbolizing Cuba were used freely to portray the roles that the artists believed Cuba was playing. In this cartoon, infant Cuba appears incapable of self-help, and the caption indicates that a niggardly Uncle Sam is doing less than his share to improve the state of the island's economic health.

43. UNCLE SAM: **I'll give you one teaspoonful, Cuby. More of it might make you sick."**
William "Billy" Ireland[?], *Columbus* (Ohio) *Dispatch*, 1902.

On May 20, 1902, the United States military occupation ended and Cuba was launched as a sovereign state. During the first year the new nation not unexpectedly faced burdensome problems but fared better than had been generally anticipated in the United States. President Tomás Estrada Palma ruled with a relatively even hand and kept congress under control so that there was an acceptable degree of political tranquility. The president's program was especially successful in the economic area, thanks in large part to favorable returns from sugar, despite the failure of the United States Congress to pass a reciprocity treaty favorable to Cuba. As a consequence, the Cuban government had funds to devote to public works, the island established its credit, and the country attracted foreign capital into several industries, notably sugar. If the artist of this cartoon was not sufficiently impressed with the prospects for the future to make his characters "White" he at least made his Black children appear competent and confident in contrast to the Black bunglers that the public had already become accustomed to associate with Cuba.

**44.  After the First Mile**

W. L. Evans[?], *Cleveland Leader*, 1903.

Despite disclaimers to the contrary, Cuba's trade with the United States grew spectacularly following its independence from Spain. But the Cuban government's share of the gain was soon being dissipated by a corrupt bureaucracy and appropriations for war veteran pensions. By 1905, the nation's early prospects for success had been seriously blighted, and in July 1906 a revolt forced the first elected regime from power. Meanwhile, Puerto Rico, under United States control, had remained relatively stable. The news media in the United States generally showed little patience when Cuba found itself in political difficulty and did not hesitate to show its hostility. In this cartoon Cuba is triply damned. It is kept a child. It is Black. And the child as a reckless gunslinger is made to play the role of an irresponsible adult.

**45.** UNCLE SAM to PORTO RICO: "And to think that bad boy came near being your brother!"
*Chicago Inter Ocean*, 1905.

Unrest in Cuba over alleged election frauds was so widespread by 1906 that President Estrada Palma requested
intervention by the United States, which sent commis-
sioners to mediate. Mediation failed. Estrada Palma resigned in July, and on September 29, the United States
proclaimed a provisional government until January 28,
1909, when the republic was reinaugurated a second
time. The insurrectionists promptly disbanded following
the creation of the provisional government and order
was restored. In this cartoon Uncle Sam is content with
his achievement and with the pacified "White" Cuba that
will have to be nursed back to self-government.

**46. The International Nurse**

THE BABY'S UNCLE: "Why, this is not such a bad child, after all."
*Baltimore News,* 1906.

The artist of this cartoon obviously doubted that the
United States would relinquish the control it held under
the provisional government formed after the downfall of
Estrada Palma. For him, "Freedom" turned out to be a
marionette presumably to be manipulated by Washington with the United States Navy in a supporting role.
Although the cartoonist faults the United States, his rendi-
tion of Cuba as childlike and innocent could have done
little to convince his viewers that the island was in reality
equipped to survive in a world of imperial powers.

**47. Cuba's Freedom Is Not Far Off**

Thomas May, *Detroit Journal,* 1907. Reprinted by permission of *The Detroit News.*

This cartoon and the preceding one appeared in the same issue of the *Review of Reviews*. Both suggest a friendliness toward the island on the part of the artists. Cuba is here neatly dressed and shows a desire to learn, and neatness and learning were highly valued by the early twentieth-century generation. But that generation also tended to be overly protective of female children. Uncle Sam for the moment is almost out of the picture.

**48.  Can She Go It Alone?**
*Toledo Blade*, 1907. Reprinted by permission of *The Blade*, Toledo, Ohio.

Charles E. Magoon was named to head the provisional government of Cuba in October 1906. He sided with the militarists who favored making Cuba a United States protectorate, an alternative opposed by both Secretary of War William Howard Taft and President Theodore Roosevelt. In 1907 the artist responsible for this cartoon had portrayed Cuba as learning to walk on the path to self-government. On this occasion, just months before the provisional government ended in January 1909, an alert Cuba was about to try once again to "go it alone" under the friendly observation of Uncle Sam.

## 49. About Ready to Walk

UNCLE SAM: "Say, Maggie, let's see if she can go it alone."

*Cleveland Leader*, 1908. Reprinted by permission of *The Plain Dealer*, Cleveland.

Nicaragua, under President José Santos Zelaya, had intervened in Honduras to oust President Policarpo Bonilla;
thereafter, the two nations had signed a treaty and were,
according to the cartoon, at peace. The cartoon blows
out of all proportion the Mexican-Guatemalan controversy which revolved around a Mexican request that a
Guatemalan army officer be extradited to stand trial on
charges of having murdered an ex-president of Guatemala on Mexican soil. The Mexican minister to Guatemala was reassigned to El Salvador and Mexican troops
moved south, but Guatemalan officials had been assured
that Mexico did not intend to push for satisfaction were
its request denied. The cartoon, thus, is a good example
of an all-too-common kind of gross misrepresentation of
developments in Latin America, sometimes out of ignorance, sometimes by intent. The cartoon is also of interest
because Mexico is portrayed as a troublesome infant at a
time when the Mexican president, Porfirio Díaz, was
highly regarded in the United States and his government
was cooperating with Washington in attempts to bring
order out of the instability that Central America was
undergoing.

**50. More Trouble in the Nursery**
Osborn, *Milwaukee Sentinel*, 1907. Reprinted by permission of the *Milwaukee Sentinel*.

This cartoon appeared in the same issue of the *Literary Digest* as the preceding one. Here the same Mexican-Guatemalan incident assumes importance because of its possible effect upon the United States role at the Second Hague Conference where the use of armed forces to collect public debts was debated. Using a minor issue to cast Guatemala and Mexico in such unattractive roles reflected at once a widely held view of Latin America in official and press circles at the time and also, presumably, the public's receptiveness to derogatory images of the republics.

**51.   The Old Man Doesn't Want the Effect Spoiled**

UNCLE SAM: "Now I am going in here to make a peace speech, and I don't want you
boys to start any rough house while I'm talkin'."

Carter, *Minneapolis Tribune*, 1907. Copyright © Minneapolis Tribune. Reprinted
by permission.

In 1909 Nicaraguan elements supported by United States–owned companies rose against dictator José Santos Zelaya. During the disturbances, two United States citizens were killed. United States marines were landed. Zelaya resigned and José Madriz was named to succeed him. Madriz was not acceptable to either the revolutionaries or Washington, and the United States denied him recognition. United States naval forces occupied the city and port of Bluefields. The United States–favored candidate, Adolfo Díaz, became president in 1911. In sum, the United States became involved in Nicaragua in the interest of United States investors there. In this cartoon, which appeared during the height of the struggle for power, the incorrect inference was that Nicaragua was to be disciplined for violating the Monroe Doctrine when in fact the issue was a strictly domestic one. Given Nicaragua's size and Uncle Sam's determination, not only was the former going to be thrashed, but his dark complexion and sullen expression would also keep him from receiving any sympathy.

**52. Cutting a Switch for a Bad Boy**
McKee Barclay, *Baltimore Sun*, 1910. Reprinted by permission of *The Sun* (Baltimore).

This cartoon appeared during the period when Cuba's prospects of avoiding full-scale United States intervention appeared dim. A "race war" waged in Oriente province led to the landing of a small contingent of United States marines at the town of Daiquirí. And an upcoming presidential election had split the dominant Liberal Party of incumbent chief executive José Miguel Gómez. This division ultimately led President Gómez to throw his support to conservative candidate Mario Menocal, who was victorious at the polls. Up to 1912, cartoonists relied heavily upon infants and inept Black children, using Southern Black colloquialisms or dialects to create the negative images of Cuban politics they sought to convey.

**53.   Golly. I've Gone an' Did It Again!**
(Apropos of Cuba's governmental troubles)
J. H. Donahey, *Cleveland Plain Dealer*, 1912. Reprinted by permission of *The Plain Dealer*, Cleveland.

The developments in Mexico that led to this cartoon are treated below ( see no. 55 ). Turmoil also reigned in Haiti. Since 1896, nine presidents had "served" and every one of them had been overthrown or killed in office. In July 1915, the government collapsed completely. The president, Vilbrun Guillaume Sam, who was attempting to rule by terror, was seized in the French legation, to which he had fled, and was torn to pieces by a mob. President Wilson, faced with war in Europe and fearful that Germany might take advantage of the chaos in Haiti to seek submarine bases there, consented to United States occupation of the republic. Uncle Sam is trying to devote his attention to Europe and hence is annoyed by the disturbance of the neighborhood "kids," although the artist has them playing "men's" games.

**54. Attending to His Correspondence**
    King, *Chicago Tribune*, 1915. Reprinted, courtesy of the *Chicago Tribune*.

The Mexican dictator Victoriano Huerta went into exile
in July 1914. The Carranza, Villa, and Zapata factions that
had opposed him could not agree on a common leadership or program. A convention at Aguascalientes in November failed to resolve their differences. Pancho Villa
and Emiliano Zapata then formed a loose alliance against
Venustiano Carranza, and before the end of the year a
civil war broke out and continued throughout the following year. United States lives and property in Mexico were
threatened repeatedly. President Wilson's refusal to use
force to bring Mexico into line did little to win him
friends. Journalists and public officials in Washington
loudly urged a tougher policy. In this cartoon President
Wilson has a defiant Mexico backed against the wall, and
a cleanup appears certain. Readers of *Harper's Weekly*
would not have had trouble associating Mexican turmoil
and banditry with the approaching need for "the Saturday
night bath." However, many of the readers undoubtedly
would have related instinctively and sympathetically to
the "Mexican" youngster had he been made only a little
more appealing.

**55. Isn't It Just About Saturday Night?**
Walter J. Enright, *Harper's Weekly*, August 28, 1915.

In October 1915, the United States extended de facto
recognition to the government of Venustiano Carranza.
Recognition not only failed to moderate Carranza's
nationalistic ardor; it also antagonized Carranza's two
major opponents, Pancho Villa and Emiliano Zapata. In
March, Villa retaliated by raiding across the border into
New Mexico. United States forces sent into Mexico to
pursue him were ordered out by Carranza on the grounds
that their presence violated Mexican sovereignty. In June
a collision with a force of Carranza's troops at Carrizal,
together with the firing on United States ships evacuating
citizens from danger zones, nearly led to war. When this
cartoon appeared, the patience of Congress with Mexico
and with President Wilson's seeming complacence in
regard to the Mexican situation had worn thin. The "civilized" (see wall plaque) appearance and demeanor of the
young people representing Cuba, the Philippines, Nicaragua, and Panama contrast sharply not only with the
dirty, obstreperous, weapon-carrying, booted Mexican
figure, but also with the more usual unfavorable presen-
tations of those four countries by cartoonists. At a more
generalized level the cartoon is notable for the several
pictorial and verbal devices the cartoonist used to indicate his likes and dislikes.

**56.  It's for His Own Good**
John T. McCutcheon, *Chicago Tribune*, 1916. © 1916 by John T. McCutcheon.
Reprinted, courtesy of the *Chicago Tribune*.

Throughout the 1910s, Cuba was plagued by financial
corruption and electoral frauds. Economically the island
was dangerously dependent on its sugar industry which
was increasingly controlled by large foreign-owned companies. A month before this cartoon appeared in the February issue of the *Review of Reviews*, General Enoch H.
Crowder was sent to Havana to advise the Cuban government. Remembering past experiences, the watchbird
could have predicted the likely outcome of continued
political disturbances on the island. The Cuban republic,
represented here by the two young, scruffy, quarrelsome
figures, was nearly twenty years old.

**57. A Little Fracas in Cuba**
Frederick O. Seibel, *Knickerbocker Press*, ca. 1921. Reprinted with permission of
*The Knickerbocker News*, Albany, N.Y.

President Plutarco Elías Calles (1924–28), shortly after assuming office, alarmed foreign-owned companies in Mexico by making retroactive the expropriation of subsoil properties, originally provided for in the Constitution of 1917. He then proceeded to launch attacks on large landholders and the Catholic church. United States oil companies demanded intervention. Roman Catholic groups in the United States organized protests. Secretary of State Frank B. Kellogg heightened tensions in the United States and anti-Yankee sentiment in Mexico by publicly declaring that "the Government of Mexico is now on trial before the world," and later charged that Soviet agents resident in Mexico were encouraging Nicaraguans to resist United States action in that country. The United States public and most officials adamantly opposed invasion and the prospect of war quickly subsided after President Calvin Coolidge appointed Dwight W. Morrow as ambassador to Mexico. If Secretary Kellogg was guilty of irresponsible diplomatic conduct, as he surely was, the cartoonist in turn can be faulted for helping to prolong the life of the always disrespectful and, by the late 1920s, overworked, practice of representing the Latin American republics in childlike roles. Nearly all artists appearing in establishment journals and newspapers were about to discard that device.

**58. Lost Something, Didn't You, Frank?**
Howard M. Talburt, *Washington News*, 1926. Reprinted by permission of the Scripps-Howard Newspaper Alliance.

Political instability provided the occasion for the return of United States troops to Nicaragua from 1926 until 1932. Throughout the occupation President César Augusto Sandino protested the United States presence. His depredations upon North Americans and his repeated embarrassment of United States marines sent in search of him won him acclaim as an anti-*yanqui* man of valor. Meanwhile, the loss of lives among marines made the occupation increasingly unpopular at home. It is noteworthy that this cartoonist assigned Nicaragua to a cradle at a time when portrayal of the republics as children was on the wane and would cease in the 1930s when the Good Neighbor Policy was pronouncing the equality of hemisphere nations. Charles Lindbergh's good will tour is discussed in chapter 3.

**59. Welcome, Lindbergh!**
Cal Alley, *Memphis Commercial Appeal*, 1928. Reprinted by permission of *The Commercial Appeal*, Memphis.

# 5. THE REPUBLICS AS BLACKS

The lynching of 162 Blacks in 1892 marked an all-time high for the United States in that category of crimes against mankind.[1] The lynchings were but one of the more outward manifestations of the full flowering of racism in the United States during the late nineteenth century. Always vulnerable to social and economic discrimination because of color and close association with chattel slavery, the Black in the decades before and during World War I was subjected to both increasingly brutal and more sophisticated forms of repression. Southern mobs by 1890 were torturing and burning their Black victims. Particularly in the South, patterns of violence against Blacks were upheld by the relative lack of fear of legal reprisals from lower courts where the pressures of a deeply prejudiced local opinion were most strongly felt, where judges were often of limited education and provincial backgrounds, and where the few Black lawyers lacked specialization to handle important cases. Outside the South, most notably in industrial areas, ghettoization and segregation were becoming more and more commonplace. Everywhere, racist demagoguery competed with condescension, paternalism, and benevolent sympathy in the imposition of an invidious group identity on all Blacks. Insolence, a lack of the most rudimentary elements of morality, the inability to share "our" democratic opportunities,[2] and an incapacity to behave in their own economic self-interest even under the best of circumstances (a view popularized by labor unions controlled by recent arrivals from Europe) were added to the already widely accepted White stereotypes of Blacks as superstitious, docile, thriftless, emotional, intemperate, unstable, dishonest, promiscuous, happy-go-lucky, and music loving. On those occasions when the race question was permitted to rise to any level of public consciousness, it was treated politically rather than morally.

Formalized racism had reached its peak of power and influence by 1920. Soon therafter it began to be challenged seriously by the emerging liberal environment. By the 1930s, industrialization, technological advances, a high level of mobility, the increasing questioning of the tenets of social Darwinism, and a growing awareness of world animadversion resulted in overt racism losing much of its credibility among the liberal intelligentsia. But if racism as a comprehensive ideology was rejected by many, prejudice as an attitude lingered on, as it still does. And that attitude manifested itself in the continuing inability of Blacks to shed their ancestry; by their failure, ordinarily, to gain access to adequate educational opportunities, good jobs, and union rights; and by their namelessness in occasional pictures appearing in textbooks—to mention just some of the areas in which Blacks were cast as unequal and inferior, thus indirectly providing psychological ammunition for those who would justify the hegemony of established social elements.

The public's determination not to examine rationally the interrelationship between the material facts and their beliefs about Blacks was too apparent and exploitable to go unnoticed by cartoonists in search of ways to direct attention to their views of Latin America. During the three decades (roughly between 1900 and 1930) that racism flourished in the United States, the cartoonists added a profoundly Black image to their repertoire of pejorative and/or patronizing characterizations of the Latin American component of the hemisphere family. Before racism as applied to Blacks fell from intellectual respectability, the cartoonists had cast as Black every Caribbean republic, with the possible exception of Costa Rica. In the process, the artists strongly reaffirmed Thomas Hobbes's conclusion "that, while any person's actual possibility to improve the lot of his fellow creatures amounted to almost nothing, everyone's opportunities to do damage was always immense."

The artists left very little to the imagination as they randomly selected from the long list of physical, oral, and social caricatures with which a prejudiced public could quickly relate. The republics were lampooned variously as cheerful, improvident, carefree Blacks, meant to recall the myth of 'the happy and contented bondsman" or the popular minstrel of an earlier age. They became unintelligent, lazy, dozing people with a consuming appetite for cigars and watermelons or gunslinging, razor-wielding rowdies. And if words were put in their mouths, those words were almost always in southern Black dialect. In brief, a black face and a foreign dialect symbolically transformed Latin America into a stereotype that paralleled the condition of, and evoked from a prejudiced White North American society the same responses as, Blacks in the United States at a time when the prevailing ethic was "keep them in their place."

The cartoonists' use of Black symbolism in portraying Latin America tells us much about their societal role. Their work shows that they waited

nearly a decade after Black racism had luxuriated before commonly ex-
ploiting it in dealing with the republics to the south. And they dropped the
practice only in 1930 when it became evident that the ideology was finally
and definitively on the defensive. This would appear to give strong support to the contention that cartoonists are purveyors rather than makers
of public opinion.

Admiral George Dewey captured Manila on May 1, 1898, and Spain's wartime resistance collapsed. Hawaii was annexed two months later. It was apparent that the United States could go the route of imperialism should it choose to do so. The pro-imperialists argued trade, mission, duty, destiny, and defense. The anti-imperialists countered that imperialist involvement would have an unfavorable influence upon the national character and that the "uncivilized" peoples of the potential colonies and protectorates could not be accorded the same rights and privileges guaranteed United States citizens by the Constitution. A major reason that the prospective colonials were held to be unqualified for full citizenship was their presumed racial origin, which Darwinism contended denied them the capability of responsibly participating in and enjoying the benefits of a government designed for "the White race." In this cartoon President McKinley ponders the merits of acquiring territories, including Cuba, considered to be inhabited by inferior peoples of non-Caucasian origins. While the president reflected, public opinion crystallized in favor of annexation of non-White peoples.

**60. The Cares of a Growing Family**

J. Campbell Cory, *New York Bee*, May 25, 1898. Courtesy of the General Research and Humanities Division; the New York Public Library; Astor, Lenox, and Tilden Foundations.

This cartoon is one artist's version of the United States'
assumption of an imperial role. The United States stand
on imperialism was significantly influenced by the British
experience. John Bull, thus, could justly claim some
credit for the decision of the United States to join the race
for new colonies in areas populated by "lesser breeds
without the law," to borrow Rudyard Kipling's words.
The British could also take some solace from the prospect of support from a strong United States in the Western penetration of the Orient. But the cartoon is of interest primarily for its depiction of the peoples, including
the Cubans, who might compose the empire. The figures
are not children, but pygmylike adults with African appearances, including earrings. The implication of inferiority is much stronger here than in the previous cartoon. Children can be educated and do grow up. These
figures are already adults, but their size will keep them
forever subordinate while their racial features are used to
indicate not only race but also lack of civilization.

61. JOHN BULL: "It's really most extraordinary what training will do. Why, only the other day I thought that man unable to support himself."
Fred Morgan, *Philadelphia Inquirer*, 1898.

Before the United States went to war with Spain, the
Cuban patriots had a favorable press in the United States,
as their struggle was made to appear as one of civilization
against Spanish barbarism. Once troops were landed in
Cuba, United States officers quickly concluded that
Spanish officers were far more honorable and civilized
than the patriots, whose treatment of prisoners and Spanish sympathizers was viewed as savage and brutal. The
officers' convictions were soon reflected in the United
States news media. As the United States view was modified, the image of the patriot changed from a light-skinned
to a dark-skinned person. When civil strife continued
after the defeat of Spain, the United States Congress
appropriated funds to be paid to ex-patriots who agreed
to lay down their arms. In this cartoon all ex-patriots are
stereotyped as improvident Blacks, quickly recovered
from their wounds (note discarded crutches), content
after receiving their share of United States largesse.

**62. This Style of Plaster Will Cure All Their Wounds**
Thomas May, *Detroit Journal*, 1899.

Once Cuba was freed from Spain, there was considerable
support in the United States press for Washington to relax
its trade restrictions against Cuban sugar and tobacco.
While the matter was before Congress the sugar and
tobacco trusts lobbied against legislation favorable to
Cuba. Though not totally effective, their effort was
sufficient to see that Congress granted fewer concessions than the pro-Cuban groups felt necessary if the new
nation was to become economically viable. This cartoon
speaks to the reciprocity issue and invites sympathy for
Cuba. Its most striking feature, however, is the use of
attributes associated with the stereotypical Black from
the rural South to portray Cuba: shabby gingham shirt,
patched overalls, tattered hat, bare feet, oversized band-
age on the injured toe, and Southern Black dialect. Com-
pare this with cartoon 53.

**63. CUBA:** "Pahdon me; but would you ge'mmen move aside so's I could get in?"
James Donahey, *Cleveland Plain Dealer*, 1902.

Despite the great temptation to stay, President Roosevelt stunned the imperialist world by withdrawing from Cuba in 1902. His decision came after the Cubans incorporated the Platt Amendment into their constitution, thus making the island a quasi protectorate of the United States. This cartoon belongs to the same genre as the preceding one and most of the others in this chapter. The exaggerated facial features, the huge cigar, and the language of the caption all invite the viewer to equate Cubans with the caricatured southern Black.

**64.** CUBA: "Yo' watch me, chile, mebbe yo' hab a chance yo'se'f some day."
Westerman[?], *Ohio State Journal* (Columbus), 1902.

President McKinley supported reciprocity with Cuba
and President Roosevelt used his influence to keep pressure on Congress in favor of fairer trading arrangements
for the island. Yet it took Congress three years to make up
its mind. Last-minute differences among the House, the
Senate, and the president resulted in postponing the
enactment of the measure into law until after this cartoon
originally appeared.

**65.** CUBA: "Well, it ought to be a good one, it's been fattening long enough."
Leip, *Detroit News*, 1903.

When Cuba achieved its independence, the status of the Isle of Pines to the south of the main island was left to future adjustment by treaty. In 1925, the United States by treaty recognized it as part of Cuba. In the meantime, United States investors and property owners on the island repeatedly sought to bring it under the United States umbrella, which already afforded protection to other dark-skinned peoples.

**66. The Isle of Pines Looking for Shelter**
*Binghamton Press*, 1905.

The incongruity of the insistence by the protagonists for imperialism that it was the obligation of the Whites to uplift the benighted, dark-skinned peoples of the Caribbean and the Pacific islands and their insensitivity to the expectancies of Afro-Americans in their midst was seldom called to the public's attention during the era of expansion. This cartoon was unusual for its time in that it spoke to that matter. It is included here to call attention to the possible unfavorable consequences for the Latin American republics of being portrayed as Black by the United States news media.

**67. Uncle Sam's Burden**

AMERICAN NEGRO: "Lift me up, too; I was here first."
*Ram's Horn* (Chicago), 1903.

On November 3, 1903, the "patriot" Panamanian army revolted against Colombian authorities. On November 4, Panama declared its independence. On November 6, the United States granted the new republic de facto recognition. President Roosevelt had surreptitiously involved the United States in the movement to separate Panama from Colombia and then guaranteed Panama's independence by posting United States naval forces off Panama City to block the advance of troops dispatched to reaffirm Colombian control. Panama for the moment could justly be considered a United States protectorate. This cartoon is one of the many that at once made Panama Black and infantile, thereby depriving it of independent judgments.

**68. A Kind Old Gentleman Is Asked to Hold a Baby for "Just a Minute"**
Walker, *Milwaukee Journal*, 1903.

On November 18, exactly two weeks after Panama claimed its independence from Colombia, the Hay-Bunau-Varilla Treaty was initiated. On February 23, 1904, the United States approved the treaty, which provided for a payment of $10 million down and $250,000 annually and gave this country extraordinary sovereign rights over a ten-mile strip across the new republic. In this cartoon the artist, while calling attention to the treaty, makes doubly sure that it is understood that in his opinion the United States was dealing with an inferior people by using a Black child with saliva dripping from the corner of his mouth in anticipation of a watermelon, which, according to the wisdom of the day, Blacks found practically impossible to resist.

**69. They Would Like to Get In**

("The islands of San Andres and Providence want to join the Panama republic."—
News item)

W. L. Evans[?], *Cleveland Leader*, ca. 1904.

Colombia resented the United States involvement on the isthmus immediately following the declaration of Panamanian independence. Not surprisingly, there were remarks made in Bogotá and elsewhere suggesting that national pride required Colombia to challenge the United States in Panama. This artist probably exaggerated the seriousness of the Colombian remarks for purposes of effect. Ridicule was a favorite device of early twentieth-century cartoonists, and how better to ridicule than to have a categorically mismatched Black square off against Uncle Sam?

70. UNCLE SAM: "If you are determined to finish me up, sail in; this suspense is something awful."

G. W. Rehse, *St. Paul Pioneer Press*, ca. 1904.

Ulíses Heureaux became president of the Dominican Republic (Santo Domingo) in 1882 and retained power until 1899, when he was killed by political enemies. His regime gave the nation badly needed peace, but at the price of corrupt despotism and reckless financial management. During the half decade after his death, weak governments rose and fell in quick succession. One of these regimes ousted the Santo Domingo Improvement Company, which after 1892, had exercised a measure of control over Dominican finances and development. Under urging from the State Department the Dominican government agreed to pay the company $4.5 million (of a claim of $11 million) in installments, and an arbitral tribunal ordered that the United States should assume control over certain customhouses if these installments were not met. Political unrest and economic irresponsibility caused European debtors to press the claims of their citizens, and intervention by Germany, France, Belgium, or Italy appeared a serious possibility. Bad as conditions were when this cartoon was published, they worsened in the months ahead. In a very large majority of cases, cartoonists portrayed the Dominican Republic as Black. This caricature not only relied heavily upon standard stereotypical Black images but also exploited the conviction in the United States that the razor was the Black man's preferred fighting weapon. The use of "boy" in the caption gives added emotional impact to the caricature.

**71.** UNCLE SAM: **"Maybe I'll have to bring the boy into the house to keep him quiet."**
G. W. Rehse, *St. Paul Pioneer Press*, 1904.

This cartoon appeared at approximately the same time as the preceding one and, like it, called attention to the United States interest in the problems facing the Dominican Republic. President Roosevelt is substituted for Uncle Sam and machetes for the razor as symbols of destructive behavior. The watermelon was, by 1904, a ready-made associational device in the cartooning of developments in the Caribbean republics.

**72.** **The Strenuous One Will Catch You, If You Don't Watch Out!**
   C. G. Bush, *New York World*, 1904.

President Roosevelt concluded that, if the United States would not permit European powers to collect debts by force, it had the "moral mandate" to intervene and compel the reluctant republics to pay their bills. That view was outlined in his annual message to Congress in December 1904, now referred to as the "Roosevelt Corollary" of the Monroe Doctrine. In the same month, Secretary of State John Hay instructed the United States minister in Santo Domingo to determine whether the Dominican president would be favorably inclined to invite the United States government to collect and distribute Dominican customs duties. Soon thereafter a treaty was signed which provided for the United States to take over the collection of customs revenues and to negotiate settlements with the republic's creditors. The United States Senate declined to approve the treaty, but Roosevelt, acting on his own responsibility, established a customs collecting system by executive order. Under United States direction, collections were considerably increased almost immediately. The neat, upright figure symbolizing Santo Domingo—one of a very few dealing with Latin American that portrayed a Black adult in a positive light—calls attention to the change which the artist considered to be for the better. Developments that influenced the cartoonist to portray Venezuela as unkempt and scrubby compared to Santo Domingo are reviewed below (see nos. 77 and 90).

**73.** **Uncle Sam Invites Venezuela to Occupy a Chair in the International Barber Shop, Just Made Vacant by Santo Domingo**
Clifford Berryman, *Washington Post*, 1905.

Despite generally better economic conditions and relief from creditors after the United States took charge of collecting and redistributing customs duties, turmoil continued to be a featured aspect of Dominican politics. This cartoon and no. 71 were drawn by the same artist. Two years of direct United States influence in the republic's fiscal affairs had not significantly changed his opinion of the Dominican people or their nation.

**74. Uncle Sam's Periodical Bad Man**

G. W. Rehse, *St. Paul Pioneer Press*, ca. 1906. Reprinted by permission of the *Dispatch/Pioneer Press*.

On February 7, 1905, President Roosevelt asked the Senate to approve the convention recently agreed to by the Dominican Republic. But enough senators had become disillusioned with expansionism, and resentful of what they considered the president's determination to increase executive power at the expense of the legislative branch, to shun the treaty. Rebuffed, Roosevelt acted on his own and put into operation the machinery to collect and dispense the island's customs duties. A modified treaty, which gave the Senate and the president chances to save face and which paid greater attention to Dominican sensibilities, was negotiated and ratified in 1907. According to this cartoon, the Black, childlike Dominicans, confronted with revolution and political instability, considered the original Roosevelt agreement worth clinging to irrespective of the temper of the Senate.

**75. Still Holding On to It**

"I knows when I's got a good thing."

*Cleveland Leader*, ca. 1906. Reprinted by permission of *The Plain Dealer*, Cleveland.

This cartoon accompanied an article in the *Literary Digest* entitled "Should the United States Intervene in South America?" The thrust of the article was that dictator Cipriano Castro of Venezuela was keeping alive hostilities between his country and Colombia and that constant unrest in the area might compel the United States to intervene to protect its interest in Panama, then a part of Colombia. Castro was satirized unmercifully in the United States press, but in no other instance did the *Literary Digest*, the *Review of Reviews*, *Harper's Weekly*, or *Puck* portray him as a Black. By using the watermelon and the reference to a "southern gentleman," the artist practically guaranteed that his image of Castro as a Black would not escape the reader.

**76. There Seems to Be a Southern Gentleman in the Melon Patch**
G. W. Rehse, *St. Paul Pioneer Press*, 1901.

The tyrant Cipriano Castro had used forces from the Andean region of Venezuela to seize control of the national government in 1899. He openly defied Venezuela's European creditors and, when this led to a blockade of the republic in 1902–03, Castro's countrymen in a display of national fervor gave him their support. President Roosevelt interceded and secured the withdrawal of the blockading fleet and arranged to have the creditors' claims adjudicated by the new international court at The Hague. When the world tribunal scaled down the claims against Venezuela, Castro was hailed as a national hero. During the remainder of his dictatorship he exploited threats from abroad to retain his hold on the country. His cavalier treatment of the Dutch ambassador resulted in the seizure of Venezuelan war vessels by The Netherlands in 1905. The artist used the dictator's lethargic warriors to accentuate his personal need for action in order to retain his domination of the nation.

77.  CASTRO: "Carambo, this suspense is killing."
Reynolds, *Tacoma Daily Ledger*, 1909. Reprinted by permission of the *Tacoma News Tribune*.

In November 1908, President Castro sailed to Europe ostensibly for medical attention, leaving in charge his ablest military officer, Juan Vicente Gómez. Gómez quickly usurped all political power, and Castro was ordered not to return to Venezuela on pain of death. The latter could not accept this turn of events and for several years moved about the Caribbean attempting to organize forces that would return him to power. Foreign nations, with some reason, refused him support, and if there were any champions of the ex-dictator within Venezuela, Gómez kept them suppressed. During the entire Castro era, cartoonists created the unavoidable impression that Venezuela was a Black nation led by a disreputable dictator.

**78. Sounds Are So Deceiving**
Thomas May, *Detroit Journal*, 1906. Reprinted by permission of *The Detroit News*.

War between Guatemala and El Salvador broke out when the military and private citizens of El Salvador gave aid to revolutionists in Guatemala bent on deposing that nation's president. Subsequently, a force of Guatemalans allegedly crossed the border into Honduras, whereupon Honduras declared war against Guatemala. Through the good offices of Mexico and the United States, differences among the three republics were settled and, as the cartoon suggests, peace reigned. El Salvador, Guatemala, and Honduras are each pictured as Black children. Given the explicit connotations of casting the republics as Black and childlike, the fact that the cartoonists did not choose faithfully to record the basically Indo-European origins of the republics becomes only secondarily important.

**79.** UNCLE SAM: **"The kids are in bed and all is well."**
*Seattle Post-Intelligencer*, 1906. Reprinted by permission of the *Seattle Post-Intelligencer*.

The dissolution of the Central American Federation in 1839 left undetermined the boundary between Nicaragua and Honduras. Resolution of conflicting claims dragged on until well into the twentieth century. Border clashes were frequent and might go unreported to the outside world. But when José Santos Zelaya, dictator of Nicaragua (1894–1909), quarreled with his neighbors, all the nations of mid-America and the United States took note. The Central American states went on the alert because the dictator aspired to unite all of Central America, by force if necessary, under his leadership; the United States was worried by his vocal opposition to Washington's intervention in Central America and the threat inherent in such unfriendliness for the United States objective of regulating all transisthmian commercial routes. Thus, when it appeared in early 1907 that clashes between Honduran and Nicaraguan forces might develop into open warfare, concern was expressed in several capitals. The artist, seeing Nicaragua and Honduras from the United States perspective, portrays them as quarrelsome black children, obviously capable of being no more than nuisances in the community of nations. The fact that Honduras had shoes indicated the artist's partiality for that side. The bear presumably referred to "Teddy" Roosevelt.

**80. A Hint**
Clifford Berryman, *Washington Star*, 1907. Reprinted by permission of the *Washington Star*.

In late 1908, Haiti experienced another of its periodic overturns in government which kept the country in a state of political and fiscal chaos. Eighty-nine–year–old Pierre Nord Alexis, president for the past six years, was the victim. Disorders in the republic prompted speculation that the United States might intervene, as it had in Santo Domingo, to bring order to Haitian politics and finances. As it turned out, the United States avoided intervention at that point, but President Wilson's "missionary diplomacy" led to the landing of marines in July 1915. The alligator as a symbol of revolution in northern Latin America was nearly as commonplace as the Black child was as an indication of political incompetence and irresponsibility.

**81. Alligator Bait**

The revolutionary alligator may swallow up little Haiti unless Uncle Sam steps in and saves the helpless child.

Thomas May, *Detroit Journal*, 1908. Reprinted by permission of *The Detroit News*.

This cartoon refers to the death of President Vilbrun Guillaume Sam and the collapse of Haiti's fragile government and financial structure in July 1915 (see no. 54). The United States promptly landed troops, presumably to preclude intervention by either France or Germany; and the Haitians were forced to sign a treaty providing for United States supervision and financial control. The worried expression on the child's face may have elicited some sympathy, but the correlation between United States intervention in the republics and their portrayal in the press as inept, simple, naïve Black children was more than accidental.

**82. I'm In for Something Now**
Hanny, *St. Joseph News-Press*, 1915. Reprinted by permission of the *St. Joseph News-Press*.

United States marines ended thirteen years of guardianship in Nicaragua in August 1925. The following year the marines were returned to that country when General Emiliano Chamorro forced a purged congress to name him president. When a restored congress designated Adolfo Díaz president, the United States hastily extended him recognition. Mexico, meanwhile, recognized Juan Bautista Sacasa, who as vice-president had fled the country at the time of the Chamorro coup. The United States and Mexican positions hardened when Washington accused the Mexican government of sending munitions to Nicaragua in support of anti-Díaz forces and of harboring communists who were giving encouragement to those in Nicaragua opposed to United States–backed parties.

This cartoon appeared at a time when Secretary of State Frank B. Kellogg was leveling a series of charges against the Calles regime in Mexico, including one that it was sheltering and providing arms to Soviet agents seeking to establish a Bolshevist government in Nicaragua. Secretary Kellogg defended the Nicaraguan intervention as necessary to prevent all of Central America from falling into communist hands. Communism was a relatively new element in United States–Latin American relations. In the view of this artist, its appearance did not alter the realities of hemispheric affairs sufficiently to cause this artist to scrap Nicaragua's standard presentation as a Black child in need of Uncle Sam's care and attention. The cartoon is of added interest because it calls attention to the perseverance of a cultural stereotype, regardless of apparent changes in the political-ideological sphere of United States foreign policy.

**83. To the Rescue!**

Craig Fox, *Rochester* (N.Y.) *Democrat and Chronicle*, 1927. Reprinted by permission of the *Democrat and Chronicle*.

By the late 1920s cartoonists, reflecting the emerging
climate of opinion that found objectionable the display
in print of slurs against certain ethnic groups, began turn-
ing away from the use of stereotypical images of Southern
Blacks to caricature unfavorably the peoples of Latin
America. But as late as 1935 when Good Neighborliness
was "in," social sensitivities still had not reached the
point where the *Review of Reviews* with its solid middle-
and upper-class following could not run approvingly this
thirty-four–year–old document with the comment,
"This cartoon of 34 years ago finds confirmation in the
inauguration of the first Filipino President in 1935." It is
telling that with very few exceptions those individuals
in the United States who in recent decades have most
significantly influenced the making and implementation
of policies affecting inter-American relations grew up
and received their formal academic training in a social
environment that would not find this cartoon an inappropriate portrayal of a Latin American people.

**84.** THE PHILIPPINES: "What yer got?"

CUBA: "Pie."

THE PHILIPPINES: "Where'd yer git it?"

CUBA: "Mah Uncle Sam gin it to me; any maybe ef you was half way decent he' gin you some."

R. C. Bowman, *Minneapolis Tribune*, 1901. Reprinted by permission from the *Minneapolis Tribune*.

# 6. THE LATIN AMERICAN NATIONS AS NON-BLACK MALES

Individuals of Iberian Catholic and Mestizo backgrounds have controlled the political, economic, and religious life of modern Latin America. The racial-religious composition of the leadership of the area has made the republics prime targets for the socially pre-eminent, race-conscious elements in the United States, who traditionally have been quick to make the transition from cultural to political ill-feeling when condemning a particular action or the general "perversity" of the nations to our south. Spaniards and Portuguese historically have been considered the least desirable of all western European peoples. That they have also been categorized as politically authoritarian and economically illiberal has provided added justification for the scorn and disdain directed toward them in the United States. And their association with the Catholic church—which has involved itself in government, engaged in such economic areas as landownership and money lending, insisted on a major role in secular education, and presumably opposed intellectual liberty—was incompatible with the ethos and institutions of North America.

Indians have fared little better. Although, after 1900, eligible for the sentimental treatment the privileged majority has been prepared to accord vanquished people, they traditionally have been denied those attributes which if developed would have qualified them for full-fledged membership in "White" society.

The low status accorded Iberians and Indians nonetheless compares favorably with that assigned the offspring of their biological "commingling." Finding support, at first, in prevailing pseudoscientific theories that held that the children of "mixed" unions inherit the worst traits of the parents and bury their virtues or, later, simply from prejudice, dominant elements in the United States have refused to grant equality to those they have classified as belonging to mixed races. Peoples led by such individuals could be acepted, if at all, for their backwardness, not for any prospects they might have for adjusting to the industrial age.

Although the United States as a whole has found the peoples and institutions of Latin America generally wanting, it has shared with the republics the phenomenon of male dominance. Having, on the one hand, recognized and accepted male "superiority" as a social reality in the republics and realizing, on the other hand, that they have been controlled by individuals of European and European-Indian origins, it is understandable that non-Black males often have been tagged as responsible for those hemispheric developments disapproved by the United States.

The non-Black male adult is the central focus of this chapter. No attempt is made to distinguish between European or "mixed" types. Racial distinctions are essentially meaningless within the Latin American cultural context since in the republics social roles are determined far more by environmental than by biological factors. Most important, cartoonists' intents often are unclear, particularly when they are dealing negatively with Latin America. This is because artists in caricaturing Caucasian and Mestizo peoples ordinarily have disregarded anthropometric and other anthropological criteria in favor of those pictorial symbols that repeated exposure has accustomed the reading public to translate quickly into terms meaningful to them: for example, diminutive and/or emaciated adults; long, stringy, black hair; unkempt dark facial hair, including mustaches; soiled clothing; bare feet; oversized huaraches; sombreros; swords; ancient rifles; bandoleers; and long cigars. On those occasions when the United States has actively sought friends in this hemisphere, for example, in times of war, cartoonists generally have cooperated by transforming the traditionally unattractive Latin American symbolic male figures into standard "Western types," but to date the transformations have not outlived the immediate concern that produced them.

A. K. Cutting, a United States citizen and editor of a newspaper in Paso del Norte, state of Chihuahua, Mexico, was arrested in Mexico in 1886 and charged with libeling a Mexican citizen. Cutting retracted the libelous statement and was released from jail. He thereupon crossed the border, reiterated the charge in print, returned to Mexico, distributed the libelous statement, and was re-arrested. The United States government, acting on incomplete reports, at first demanded Cutting's release on the grounds that he was being held in Mexico for an act committed in the United States, which in the view of the State Department amounted to a claim of extraterritorial power on the part of Mexico. The state of Texas added to the heat of the controversy when its governor declared that his forces would move if Washington failed to insist on satisfaction. United States demands were softened when the State Department accepted Mexico's position, that it was acting on the basis of the original libel committed in Mexico and Cutting's failure to carry out the "reconciliation." This "international incident" finally was settled amicably.

The cartoon perhaps is more noteworthy than the affair itself, since the artist, the incomparable Thomas Nast, as early as 1886 was making use of the numerous artistic devices widely employed over the next half century and still occasionally exploited to fashion unfavorable images of Mexico and Mexicans: superfluity of weapons, menacing attitudes, small stature, dark skin, bristly black facial hair, sombrero, and bell towers dominating the landscape.

**85. It's "Cutting"**

UNCLE SAM: "I must demand his release as an American citizen. I would much rather you would keep him, but law is law."

Thomas Nast, *Harper's Weekly*, August 14, 1886.

Brazilian Emperor Pedro II was forced into exile in 1889, bringing to an end his half century of benign if unprogressive rule; a republic was established under the nation's military leaders. During Dom Pedro's tenure the country experienced an unusual degree of political stability and public order, but the emperor and the statesmen around him failed to grasp the growing importance of civilian elements tied to Brazil's rapidly expanding coffee culture and in turn to the North Atlantic trading community. The military men who succeeded Pedro were as little attuned as the emperor had been to what was transpiring economically. Consequently, quick and widespread discontent followed his departure. By 1893 that discontent was translated into open rebellion when army units revolted in the south and were joined by naval units stationed in Rio de Janeiro. There followed some eight months of civil war before the government could restore order. During the height of the strife the United States, France, Italy, Great Britain, and Portugal kept warships in Brazilian waters and Admiral Andrew E. K. Benham, commander of the United States fleet there, gave protection to the United States merchantmen discharging their cargoes in Rio de Janeiro. Thus, although the only reference to civil disorder, other than this art and poetry to appear in the December 20 number of *Puck*, was a brief comment on British editorializing on bombings by anarchists in France, it is fair to assume that, given the United States government's direct involvement in the Brazilian conflict, the United States informed public had some notion of what was occurring in Brazil.

The cartoon and verse provide interesting evidence in support of the thesis of this work. First, although one must accept that the verse refers to Brazil, since Rio de Janeiro is the only place name mentioned, the tasseled sombrero, sash, and machete make the cartoon figure far less Brazilian than stereotypically Spanish American. Second, the cartoon figure, taken in conjunction with others published in journals directed to the reading public before and after it appeared, leaves no doubt that an abundance of black hair, mustaches, sashes, sombreros, and machetes had become standard devices for signalling attention to political disorder in Latin America generally.

E WAS a sturdy patriot,
  And he wore a big sombrero;
And he carried a wicked knife, and lived
  In Rio de Janeiro.

He did n't neglect his regular work —
  You could n't say that about him;
But no revolution could be said
  To be complete without him.

Whenever his daily toil was o'er
  He 'd be plunged in deep dejection,
Unless he happened to have a date
  To attend an insurrection.

But he married a beautiful dark-eyed girl,
  A flower of the Equator,
And she kicked whenever he did n't get home
  Until half-past two, or later.

Now, when the "*vivas*" rend the skies
  At midnight, he 's grim and surly,
For he can't take in any *coup d'état*
  Unless it finishes early.

So he 's retired from public life,
  And he grieves that his country may be
Lost for the want of his trusty sword
  While he walks the floor with the baby.
                                    *W. M.*

**86.  Suppressed**
  *Puck*, December 20, 1893.

General Máximo Gómez y Báez was a hero of the Cuban uprising of the 1870s and a leading chieftain of the anti-Spanish forces of the 1890s. A favorite of United States representatives in Cuba before and after the Spanish-American War, General Gómez refused the honor of being the new nation's first president with the words, "Men of war, for war . . . and those of peace, for peace."

The cartoon employs several techniques commonly used by political cartoonists to indicate approbation and disapprobation. The sedate, studious, proper young ladies symbolizing Hawaii and Puerto Rico as diligent students in the art of self-government being taught by Uncle Sam are neatly groomed. General Gómez, also a dedicated learner, is light skinned, his hair trimmed and neatly combed, his clothes clean, his boots polished, and his posture correct—badges of approval. By contrast, the dunce, Emilio Aguinaldo, guerrilla leader who fought first against Spain and later (1898–1901) against the United States for the independence of the Philippines, and the squabbling, perverse Cuban ex-patriot and guerrilla have swarthy skins; stringy, black messy hair; and bare feet—all marks of disparagement.

**87. Uncle Sam's New Class in the Art of Self-Government**
William Allan Rogers, *Harper's Weekly*, August 27, 1898.

Shortly after his inauguration for a second term, President McKinley made a major tour of the United States. One of his stops was at El Paso, Texas, where it was expected that he and President Porfirio Díaz of Mexico would meet on the international bridge connecting the two countries. The caption of the cartoon, "A Great Day for Old Mexico," referred to the anticipated meeting and what it would mean for Mexico. At the last moment Díaz failed to appear, on the grounds that the Mexican congress was in session and his presence in the capital was required. Díaz' personal envoy, General Juan Hernández, and McKinley exchanged greetings and promises of future cordial relations. The distinguished, manly, almost Anglo-Saxon appearing figure representing Díaz, who, as noted above, was widely admired in the United States, is in sharp contrast to his dwarflike, clownish countrymen, who more nearly fitted the prevailing image of Latin Americans.

**88. A Great Day for Old Mexico**
William Allan Rogers, *Harper's Weekly*, May 11, 1901.

Washington's negotiations first with Colombia and later with Panama for the isthmian canal route, administration of the completed waterway, and auxiliary operations produced one of the most infamous sequences of events in the history of United States–Latin American relations. Theodore Roosevelt was the central figure in the negotiations after May 1902, when the United States decided in favor of Panama over Nicaragua for the proposed route of the canal. Roosevelt's secretary of state, Hay, extracted a treaty (signed January 22, 1903) from Colombia's chargé in Washington, Tomás Herrán. Three days later Herrán received instructions from Bogotá not to sign, but the die had been cast. The United States Senate approved the treaty on March 17. The Colombian senate, objecting to the treaty on the grounds that certain provisions impinged upon the nation's sovereignty and that the financial terms were unsatisfactory, voted unanimously against ratification on August 12, 1903. There were, however, rumors suggesting that, if the United States' initial offer of $10 million was increased to $25 million, ratification would be forthcoming. At that point, if not before, Roosevelt took charge personally, and thereafter the issue moved swiftly to a "solution." On November 3, the US *Nashville* arrived off Colón, and Panamanian insurgents reasoned correctly that it was there to forestall the landing of marine reinforcements from Colombia. On November 4, Panama declared its independence. Two days later the United States granted it de facto recognition. On February 23, 1904, a treaty more favorable to the United States than the one with Colombia was ratified.

During the months of intense bargaining with Colombia, Roosevelt convinced himself that official cupidity was at the bottom of what he considered Bogotá's dalliance. On one occasion he compared Colombian behavior to that of a road agent trying to hold up a man, and this presumably explained the caption of the cartoon which appeared soon after Washington guaranteed Panama's independence. The figure representing Colombia capsulized a long-held view of Latin American politicians generally and provided a commentary on Colombian officials that was readily acceptable to the United States public.

**89. Held Up the Wrong Man**
William Allan Rogers, *Harper's Weekly*, November 21, 1903.

Cipriano Castro, as noted in chapter 5, seized control of war-torn Venezuela in 1899. For nine years he held the nation in the grip of a regime which featured continuous plundering of the treasury and gross internal mismanagement. In foreign affairs he courted disapprobation and earned a well-deserved reputation as an incorrigible international troublemaker.

The United States became actively involved in Venezuela's controversies with its creditors—notably Germany, Great Britain, and Italy—through President Roosevelt's efforts to arbitrate their disputes. Roosevelt held, first, that foreign powers possessed the right to intervene forcibly to collect legitimate debts and, second, that to avoid such possible courses of action in the Caribbean the United States must guarantee the fiscal responsibility of the republics in that area (the Roosevelt Corollary to the Monroe Doctrine).

There is no rational defense of Castro's self-serving behavior, but neither can one find in international law a reasonable justification for the United States' claiming the unilateral right to determine the norms of international conduct in this hemisphere.

The cartoon is of interest because it calls attention to one of the many roles cartoonists assigned Uncle Sam in the Caribbean and also because the artist made such excellent use of further symbols associated with presumed political irresponsibility, notably small stature, evident mental confusion, and witlessness.

**90. Uncle Sam as an Optician**
"Can you read the small print, Mr. Castro?"
Satterfield, *Cleveland Press*, 1905.

The power structure upon which the long-lived Porfirio
Díaz regime rested was an empty shell by 1910. It cracked
under the first attacks of revolutionary groups opposed
to the dictator and before those groups were compelled
to agree upon a unified set of objectives as a precondition
of victory. As a consequence, the moderate Francisco
Madero assumed control over a badly divided nation.
Elements within the national army, which were permitted to remain intact after Díaz sailed for Europe, took
advantage of the discord and of Madero's limited political
capabilities and seized the government in February 1913;
General Victoriano Huerta assumed the presidency. His
usurpation set in motion a power struggle that plunged
the nation into a succession of crises over the next several
years. In his portrayals of Madero, the army, and the un-
identified emerging presidential figure, the artist incorporated techniques that had become accepted through
repetition by the profession for caricaturing Latin American adult "White" males. Cartoonists, however, very
rarely gave identifiable figures nonhuman features of the
kind that this artist used in his depiction of Huerta.

**91. The Wheel of Fortune**

James Donahey, *Cleveland Plain Dealer*, 1913. Reprinted by permission of *The Plain Dealer*, Cleveland.

As battles raged in northern Mexico between the forces of the debauched dictator Huerta and the capricious *caudillo* Pancho Villa, there was an exodus of women, children, soldiers, and civilians across the Rio Grande into Texas. Total figures for the number that fled north are unknown, but the press reported four thousand refugees in El Paso being cared for by the War Department at government expense. The artist of this cartoon predicted that when United States generosity became known in the south there would be mass desertions, making pointless the continued military struggle for control of the nation. His refugees fit the "Latin type" too neatly not to have raised questions in the minds of some about the merits of the United States government hosting a flood of refugees as opposed to sending forces into Mexico to protect United States lives and property. When the United States army under John J. Pershing crossed the border in early 1916 in pursuit of Pancho Villa, the concept of force triumphed over that of the dole.

**92. Conquering Mexico**

William "Billy" Ireland, *Columbus* (Ohio) *Dispatch*, 1914. Reprinted by permission of the *Columbus Dispatch*.

As viewed from Washington, the United States experienced little but frustration in matters relating to Latin America during 1915. Cuba, where the United States was striving to guarantee a degree of political stability, was once again on the verge of a revolt against an incumbent regime. The Haitian government was in a state of collapse despite Washington's efforts to bring some order into the political arena. Continuing unrest in the Dominican Republic was about to lead to United States occupation of that island republic. Venezuelan dictator Juan Vicente Gómez was finding Germany's predominant political and military philosophies more congenial than those of the United States. Rooseveltian Republicans were resentful that Wilsonian Democrats were prepared to grant major concessions to Colombia in an effort to make amends for the United States role in the Panamanian revolution of 1903. And the opening of the Panama Canal had not brought with it the era of good feeling and trust that Washington had anticipated.

Relations with Mexico proved the most exasperating of all. War had narrowly been averted after the Tampico incident and the subsequent occupation of Veracruz by the offer of mediation from Argentina, Brazil, and Chile. But while diplomats talked, nationalism crested in Mexico and no leader could survive a public acceptance of the terms laid down by the mediators.

This cartoon spoke to the general state of affairs rather than to any specific country or event. The role of "policeman of the Caribbean" was proving to have annoying aspects. The absolute contrasts in size and power of the principals left little doubt of how the artist and, presumably, the public viewed the area's conduct and its place in the total context of the national interest of a United States seriously threatened by a war in Europe.

**93.** Walter Enright, *Harper's Weekly*, October 2, 1915.

Nicaragua was a major trouble spot for the United States throughout the two decades after 1912. Marines were stationed in the capital city, Managua, from that date until August 3, 1925, when they were withdrawn following the election of 1924 and the installation of a United States-approved regime. At the time this country believed that political stability had become reasonably well assured. Nonetheless, even after the withdrawal of troops, Washington kept some citizens in important positions in the Nicaraguan government, as, for example, in the overseeing of expenditures and customs receipts.

Conservative General Emiliano Chamorro seized power three months after the marines departed, but Washington refused recognition, the major factor in his early resignation. The Nicaraguan congress then elected Adolfo Díaz, who was recognized by the State Department despite opposition in the Senate led by William Borah, chairman of the Foreign Relations Committee. At the personal request of Díaz, President Calvin Coolidge landed several thousand marines. The United States forces supervised an election in 1927 and again in 1932 and the last contingents, their safety constantly threatened by the guerrilla leader General César Augusto Sandino, withdrew in 1933.

At the height of Nicaragua's political instability in the mid-1920s, Mexico threw its support to anti–United States elements. Mexico's involvement in Nicaragua came at a time when President Plutarco Elías Calles' policies over land, petroleum, and the Catholic church were contributing to a conspicuous deterioration in United States–Mexican relations. Thus, few were surprised when Secretary of State Frank B. Kellogg insisted that Calles' "socialist" administration had intervened in Nicaragua at the instigation of Moscow. Jingoists in the United States talked of war with Mexico, and President Calles heatedly denied that Moscow was behind Mexico's support of anti–United States groups in Nicaragua; when calmer minds began to prevail in Washington, concern over possible communist "mischief making" quickly subsided.

This cartoon, one of ten dealing with the Nicaraguan question in the February 1927 issue of *Review of Reviews*, is less notable for its casting of Mexicans and Nica-

**94. The Trouble Is as Close to Him as His Own Coat-tails**
William "Billy" Ireland, *Columbus* (Ohio) *Dispatch*, 1927. Reprinted by permission of the *Columbus Dispatch*.

raguans as well as communist types as undesirable troublemakers—for that was a generally accepted view in the late 1920s—than for its calling attention to an early, if mild, case of hysteria with the realization that the new communist regime in Moscow might possess the capability of agitating against the United States in its presumed sphere of influence.

The issue of *Review of Reviews* in which this cartoon appeared reported that Chicago had had more bad publicity than any other community in the world. And with some reason! It was there during the 1920s that professional gangsters and corrupt politicians cooperated to terrorize the populace while blackmailing the public and raiding municipal and county treasuries. The lives and property of those who spoke out against the insiders were publicly threatened. In the weeks before the April 10, 1928, primary election—to which the cartoon alludes—acts of intimidation ranged from assassinations, kidnappings, bombings, and machine gunnings to hundreds of small-arms attacks. It was assumed that scores of fraudulent ballots would return incumbents to office. As it turned out, when the votes finally were counted, reformist candidates made important gains, but there was in no sense a thorough political cleansing.

César Augusto Sandino was a Nicaraguan guerrilla leader who, depending on one's point of view, had gained admiration or opprobrium during the several years that he eluded captivity while harassing and embarrassing United States marines stationed in his homeland. It was a striking commentary on conditions in Chicago and Nicaragua that the artist would imply even in good humor that Sandino and his followers might add a note of respectability to a Chicago election.

**95. Sandino Comes to Chicago**

Gale, *Los Angeles Times*, 1928. Copyright, *Los Angeles Times*. Reprinted by permission.

The essence of the Good Neighbor Policy was that the
United States would abandon intervention in Latin America and make economic concessions to the nations of the
area in return for their confidence and good will. It can
be argued whether the policy began under Presidents
Calvin Coolidge, Herbert Hoover, or Franklin D. Roosevelt. That Roosevelt popularized the concept and that the
United States benefited most from it during the Rooseveltian years is certain. There were meaningful economic
and political reversals during the Good Neighbor era, but
there were only token changes in the vast area of human
relationships. United States citizens continued to consider their culture superior and themselves capable of a
great beneficence. Latin Americans continued to be
viewed as incompetent, troublesome, dependent poor
relations or simply as clients. The accompanying cartoon
reflects a popular view of Latin America held in the
United States. It ignores the declarations of equality made
during the early stages of the Good Neighbor Policy.
Latin America is stereotypically portrayed as a recipient
of United States largesse and seemingly incapable of
offering anything in return. There is in fact no more suggestion of equality or of movement in that direction than
had appeared in an overwhelming majority of cartoons
dating from the late nineteenth century.

**96.  Neighborly Call**

Pease, *Newark Evening News*, 1934. Reprinted by permission of the *Newark Evening News*.

Fidel Castro's victory over Fulgencio Batista and his alliance with the USSR brought anticommunism to a fever pitch in the United States. Communists were charged with creating trouble throughout the hemisphere and of promoting antipathy toward the United States. The stepped-up attack on the international communist apparatus served to conceal the reality that anti–United States feeling in Latin America derived largely from Washington's failure since World War II to offer Latin Americans anything more innovative than austerity as a way out of their social and economic dilemmas. This artist seemingly accepted the official Washington view that communism rather than inadequate national development was at the root of the area's unrest and of worsening hemispheric relations. In making a stereotypical Latin American farm laborer—obviously ill equipped intellectually and economically to cope with ideological propaganda—the target of communist influence, the cartoon exploited the United States image of Latin Americans as unlikely to recognize what was good for themselves in any ideological showdown.

**97. Raising Cane?**
Franklin Morse, *Los Angeles Mirror-News*, 1959. Copyright, 1959, Times Mirror
Company. Reprinted by permission.

President Eisenhower made a hurried trip to Latin America in early 1960 as a move to counter the possible political consequences of the growing respect in the area for the technological and economic capabilities of the USSR and, especially, its new diplomatic base on the shores of Latin America. The president's repeated emphasis on United States willingness to assist the republics' development and his promise of nonintervention appeared to produce an atmosphere conducive to mutually profitable inter-American cooperation. This cartoon, in one sense, captures the spirit of the time but, in another sense, the sombreroed, seraped, torpid "Latin" figure too closely resembles the stereotypical image of Latin America to give the perceptive viewer much hope that "Brotherhood Week" would last.

**98. Brotherhood Week!**
Jim Dobbins, *Boston Herald American*, 1960. Reprinted with the permission of
*The Boston Herald American*.

This 1962 cartoon hit hard and brilliantly at the phenomenon of Castro's dependence upon the USSR and his administration's difficulties in providing for Cuba's population. But to make his points, the artist relied upon those devices that have served to perpetuate the traditional disparaging image of Latin Americans as ragtag, unaspiring "have nots."

**99. Technically Speaking—We Never Had It So Good**
Ed Valtman, *Hartford Times*, 1962. Reprinted by permission of Ed Valtman.

A central theme of political cartoonists dealing with Latin America has been that the people of the area do not readily grasp the more profound significance of their actions or reactions. Thus, before World War I, President Roosevelt instituted his Big Stick policy because it was held that the fiscal irresponsibility of the Caribbean republics invited intervention by European powers which might remain entrenched after their immediate objectives were satisfied. During World War I, it was believed that President Venustiano Carranza of Mexico flirted with Germany without appreciating the full consequences of his actions. During World War II, Argentina's tolerance of Axis activities within its borders was considered to pose a dire threat to Argentina's sovereignty and to the hemisphere's security. When the Organization of American States was not moved to act against Castro's Cuba as readily as Washington wished, Latin American dilatoriness was seen as endangering the hemisphere, the point of this cartoon. What does not come through in this and other negative cartoons of the Alliance for Progress era is what was expected to be gained by portraying supposedly friendly nations as such sorry characters that they would be incapable of sustained action on their own behalf were they for some reason to make the initial effort.

**100. Why Theese Excitement? Eet's Just a Wooden Horse!**
   William Sanders, *Greensboro Daily News*, 1962. Reprinted by permission of *The News*.

The Alliance for Progress was initiated at a time when Congress was closely scrutinizing "foreign aid" budgets. In view of the Congress' attitude toward the public financing of overseas projects, its early appropriations for the Alliance were considered impressive. Still they were not so generous as had been anticipated by firm advocates of the project, and by the third year there was a sharp decline in available public funds. This cartoon calls attention to the drying-up process and also avoids the stereotyping of the recipients of aid. But, intentionally or otherwise, it also gives the erroneous but popular impression that recipients were living off handouts from the United States government, when in fact it was understood from the first that United States contributions to Latin American developmental projects under the Alliance for Progress would be supplemental, constituting a small percentage of the total costs.

**101. From Now On It'll Be Skimmed**
Bill Mauldin. © 1963. Reprinted by permission of Bill Mauldin.

No serious follower of hemispheric affairs doubted that when Lyndon B. Johnson took over from the assassinated President Kennedy the character of the Alliance for Progress and relations with Latin America generally would be modified, as in fact they were. The limited coherence that the Alliance for Progress had given United States Latin American policy was lost as the new president relaxed pressures on diverse interest groups with selfish pressures in Latin America. The Johnson stance could be explained partially in terms of the Vietnam conflict, but there is also a body of evidence which suggests that Johnson held the United States' neighbors to the south in even lower regard than did the United States public generally. The image of Latin America that the public was receiving from the press is well capsulized in this cartoon figure with his outsized sombrero, long black hair, droopy mustache, elbows on the bar, and longing look of anticipation.

**102. New Barman**

Peb, *Philadelphia Inquirer*, 1963. Reprinted by permission of *The Philadelphia Inquirer*, 1963.

The economic situation in Latin America was indeed precarious in 1964, when this cartoon appeared. The republics, already uncertain about Castro's intentions and capabilities, were struggling unsuccessfully to avoid another cycle of military dictatorships. Terms of trade in international markets were running strongly against them. Privileged elements, with their feet firmly implanted in the past, were resisting social change with all the resources at their command. Latin America was low on the Johnson administration's list of priorities, and, as the cartoon correctly suggests, conditions in the republics, figuratively speaking, were being viewed from afar by decision makers in Washington. If one were convinced that it was to the advantage of the peoples of Latin America for the United States to have a deep and abiding concern for their welfare—a conviction not universally shared—there were plenty of reasons for seeing conditions as near catastrophic: inefficient agriculture, large military budgets, poorly qualified civilian bureaucrats, and rapidly expanding populations requiring huge outlays for education and public welfare. This artist directed attention away from his stereotypical representation of Latin America but nonetheless left the impression that, if the Latin Americans were to be saved, the saving would not be by themselves but by Washington.

**103. We're Taking a New Look at It**

Herblock, *Washington Post*, 1964. Copyright 1964 by Herblock in the *Washington Post*. Reprinted by permission of Herblock Cartoons.

By the fifth year of the Alliance for Progress there were good reasons to question where the project had been and where it was going. President Kennedy had warned against expecting miracles, and there had been none. Determination and hope that had initially been shared by much of the hemisphere had given way to disinterest in the United States and despair in Latin America. Responsible figures in Washington could no more identify with any certainty where there had been lasting achievements or where failures had been repeated than could the non-contributing sombreroed, mustachioed "Latin type" in this cartoon.

**104. Where Are We?**
Ed Valtman, *Hartford Times*, 1968. Reprinted by permission of Ed Valtman.

President Richard M. Nixon gave hemisphere problems scant attention, partly reflecting his personal bias toward the area and its people but primarily because he believed that the future welfare of the United States would be determined ultimately by extrahemisphere developments. Benign neglect caused numerous Latin American officials, conditioned to periodic injections of United States capital, to suffer withdrawal pains. It can be argued whether or not it is any longer to Latin America's advantage to continue to accept at the asking price the kinds of assistance the United States is prepared to offer. But it cannot be argued that there is in this day and age anything for the United States public to gain in continuing to deny Latin Americans—as is done in this cartoon—the physical and mental equipment they will need if they are to make it on their own.

**105. Mao's Chop Suey**

Jim Yep, *Chicago Daily News*, February 24, 1972. Reprinted by permission of the *Chicago Daily News*.

In terms of impact upon the quality of national life, Mexico is today for the United States the most important country in the world. It is no less true that no country in the world is more important to Mexico than is the United States, and it is unlikely that the importance of one to the other will change significantly in the foreseeable future.

Within months after President Jimmy Carter and President José López Portillo took office in January 1977 and December 1976, respectively, two long-range issues raised relations between Mexico and the United States to a much higher level. The first was a growing awareness in the United States that annually, for well over a decade, from one to two million Mexican laborers had been illegally crossing the border. The second was the realization that a sizeable part of Mexico is floating on a sea of recently discovered gas and petroleum even as the United States searched frantically for new and reliable energy sources.

Although there were other issues, it was in the context of emigration and oil that the two presidents met in mid-February 1979. The time had come for the two nations to begin to confront those issues. Mexico could no longer expect the United States to absorb its export of labor without limit. The United States could not expect to cut the flow of illegal entries or promote the flow of petroleum and gas from Mexico without a willingness to meet its economically and politically shaky neighbor on equal terms.

President Carter flew to Mexico City prepared to deal with his Mexican counterpart as an equal—the first United States–Mexican meeting of any kind that could be said to have taken place in such an atmosphere. Although there is some evidence to the contrary, it is probable that the meeting of the presidents helped to clear the diplomatic air somewhat. Still the sessions made abundantly evident that the two countries face serious challenges in their future relations. The United States has much to learn before it consistently responds with maturity to changes taking place in Mexico. For its part, Mexico must more fully appreciate that its petroleum reserves at best give it only short-range domestic and international maneuverability. When its oil and gas are depleted, the United States presumably will remain.

This cartoon, supposedly depicting the welcoming

**106.** Ed Valtman, *Hartford Times*, 1979. Reprinted by permission of Ed Valtman.

ceremonies, is remarkable for several reasons. There are no sombreros, serapes, cacti, or unkempt drooping mustaches; the two presidents' left hands suggest the underlying urgencies—assistance and oil—of the meeting. The artist does not have the presidents' eyes meet, as if anticipating that they would talk past one another in forthcoming sessions, as they did a good deal of the time. The presidents' stature and apparel suggest equal status that in fact characterized the meetings and should prevail in the future. Mexico is not a "pipsqueak country" as syndicated columnist Andrew Tully gratuitously labeled it in a March 1979 release.[1] To so portray it is tantamount to performing a disservice to both Mexico and the United States.

# 7. SOCIAL REFORM AND MILITARISM

Of the many hundreds of cartoons on hemispheric topics that appeared in United States newspapers and periodicals during the century ending in 1960 and subscribed to by the "informed public," only a scattering attempted to place on the record the social and military-political environments that were so profoundly influencing the domestic affairs and international conduct of the Latin American republics. Readers, as a consequence, learned of developments characteristically associated with political and economic instability; they were not informed of the cultural, social, and economic chasms that separated the privileged few from the submerged many and thus of the dissidence that echoed throughout the hemisphere. Seldom indeed were readers informed by the artists that the seeming political capriciousness actually reflected the very basic fact that little land was owned by the mass of peasants who constituted the economic backbone of several of the nations or of the burdens of inequitable distribution of income largely carried by urban laborers. Nor did the cartoonists associate social alienation with the quite limited opportunities for education and the scant public funds allocated to social welfare. Armed violence was pictorialized repeatedly but, with remarkably few exceptions, the perpetrators were *bandidos* or *guerrilleros* rather than the national military establishments. The apparent sanctity of the military may be assumed to have resulted at times from a dearth of objective information or interest, but at least it seems equally apparent that the armed forces often escaped the cartoonist's brush because they had associated themselves with either the elite civilian or the personalist regimes approved by Washington.

But if cartoonists for a century largely ignored social issues and the national military establishments, that circumstance changed with the launching of the Alliance for Progress in the early 1960s. Certain cartoonists caught the new spirit and capsulated for their followers the flood of propaganda pouring out of Washington on the political, economic, and social conditions in Latin America considered to be in urgent need of modification. Although they customarily continued to treat Latin America as a monolith rather than a community of individual and unique nations, by alerting the public to the fact that our neighbors to the South suffer chronic institutional illnesses, they undoubtedly made a contribution to inter-American understanding. Their contribution would have been even greater had the artists been less inclined to follow the lead of the instant experts on Alliance for Progress payrolls who cast the republics' social problems in dichotomous rich-or-poor, order-or-chaos, reform-or-revolution terms and had their art focused more on the issues of political economy and less on political leadership per se in Latin America. If the history of Latin America teaches anything, it is that throughout the area the institutional changes take place slowly and grudgingly when at all, the Cuban experience notwithstanding.

As the cartoons in this chapter make clear, since the early 1960s artists have taken a strong stand against the institutionalized armed forces. I hope that the legends accompanying the cartoons make equally clear that, while the artists have helped to keep before the public a disturbing political phenomenon in Latin America, they have left as much unsaid about the armed forces as they have said. The artists are to be faulted in two areas in particular. First, they have failed to note that most Latin American governments are fused coalitions, and, as a consequence, it is unrealistic to make rigid distinctions between the military and civilian spheres. Second, in so forcefully associating the armed forces with the republics' social-economic backwardness, the cartoonists have tended to absolve civilian politicians of their very large share of responsibility for the unsatisfactory social-economic conditions of the popular elements they have so thoroughly dominated.

At least two major conclusions may be drawn from cartoons 107–119. First, contemporary cartoonists are paying closer attention to internal conditions in Latin America than did their predecessors. Second, they still too often resort to the century-long tradition of portraying Latin America at its worst, presumably to satisfy the images and needs of their particular following.

Two considerations recommended that social issues and the centralized armed forces be treated in a single chapter. The first is that in terms of numbers they represent a quite small percentage of the total output of cartoons dealing with Latin America. To have allotted each topic a chapter would have tended to distort their relative importance, given the historical context of the volume. The second consideration is that political problems born of unsatisfactory social environments have been used repeatedly by the armed forces to justify intervention in the civilian area, either on their own account or as spokesmen for the classic corporate structure.

As Figures 120 through 131 suggest, artists have treated the Latin
American armed forces on basically three levels. Initially, they were nearly always portrayed as buffoons, although not unusually greedy and irresponsible buffoons, of the variety that "one might expect in banana republics." By the 1940s, the military was more often cast as posing a threat
to civilian democratic rule, as was appropriate for an "informed public"
which continued to believe that a United States–fashioned democracy
offered the surest route to resolving the world's problems. Beginning in
the 1960s, the political artists in general shifted their emphasis in order
to bring their views more into line with the goals of the Alliance for Progress, and the institutionalized armed forces became *the* institution block-
ing the way to the reforms that Washington contended would finally
launch Latin America on the road to modernity.

The decade after 1900 was a tumultuous one for Mexico. Strikes (and their ferocious suppression), rural disorders, food shortages, the disaffection of leading intellectuals, and the frustrations of Mexican businessmen in the commercial and industrial sectors where foreigners and foreign products were favored by the government were some of the early symptoms of the illness that finally seized the nation during the election of 1910. The aging Porfirio Díaz was the immediate source of the republic's torment. Not only had he again offered himself as the official presidential candidate (which was tantamount to election) but he had also insisted on naming his running mate, thereby precluding for the foreseeable future any reasonable expectation of escape from a political system that had kept the social and economic order suspended in time. Predictably, Díaz and his vice-presidential choice won office, but this time the disparate opposition groups refused to be still. Under mounting pressure from makeshift armies, the regime toppled and the dictator went into exile in May 1911. His departure set in motion the second phase of the civil war, one that would rend the republic for the next half decade.

Contemporary observers in the United States generally viewed the conflict as another in the long series of power struggles in Latin America, meaningful only to the degree that it might affect United States interests in the region. But the conflict outstripped this presumption primarily because industrial workers and agrarian elements, the historical victims of a vicious landholding system and its corollary, peonage, kept the contest alive until it was given a social content to be officially acknowledged in the Constitution of 1917.

But while other cartoonists stuck to traditional themes, centering their attention on the political and international matters created by the revolutionary armies fighting variously under the banners of Venustiano Carranza, Pancho Villa, Emiliano Zapata, and a host of lesser figures, the artist of this cartoon identified the very basic cause of the torment for which tens of thousands were laying down their lives. What inspired him but escaped the others is unknown. It could have been John Kenneth Turner's *Barbarous Mexico* (1911), which exposed in graphic and colorful terms the human misery, avarice,

**107. What Is the Matter with Mexico?**
Barnett, *Los Angeles Tribune*, 1913.

and brutality suffered by the masses, especially the Yaquí and Maya Indians of Sonora and Yucatán, respectively. Or he may have had access to some of the thousands who fled to the United States and who knew better than any United States journalist what conditions were like in Mexico. Whatever the source or sources of his concern, his sensitivity and perceptiveness in capturing the essence of the struggle that engulfed Mexico make the cartoon perhaps the most unusual and noteworthy ever to appear on hemispheric matters.

It could be said that in this century the history of Mexico has been largely the history of land and those who possessed it. The ownership of land, whether by the Catholic church, the *hacendado*, the foreigner, the peasant village, the Mexican nation, or the *ejidatario* (a small holder allotted land to which the government retains title), has been an overriding issue. It was a major question of the Revolution of 1910. Land redistribution has been a stated major objective of the monolithic Institutional Revolutionary Party (PRI) since its founding in 1929. Yet today, matters relating to the land repeatedly capture the headlines.

This cartoon, both less artistic and more encompassing, ran a year after the preceding one. The artist employed the same basic concept as did his colleague but moved a step beyond him explicitly to relate social injustice to political irresponsibility, represented here by President-dictator Victoriano Huerta. It is worth recalling that more than half a century later landownership remains at or very near the heart of social unrest in all of rural Latin America, except possibly in Cuba and Panama.

**108. The Real Mexican Government and the Cause of All Revolution**
Kemble, *Leslie's Illustrated Weekly*, 1914.

The Alliance for Progress, the Kennedy administration's response to the rise of Fidel Castro, traveled a near impossible obstacle course before it ground to a halt during the Johnson administration. This artist chose to label the obstacles "feudalism." His choice of a term could be challenged on a number of grounds, but suffice it to say that to apply a term rightly identified with a medieval institution to a modern state is inherently dangerous. But what is considerably more important are the questionable inferences that almost of necessity must be drawn from the cartoon. The first inference is that Latin America was still living in the middle ages, which simply was not true. Since feudalism was, first of all, a rural social-economic institution, albeit with political and juridic overtones, the second inference is that the barriers to progress, as progress was conceived of by the sponsors of the Alliance, were rural in origin. To be sure, some rural institutions were notoriously retrograde, for example the huge, inefficient, largely self-contained haciendas on which archaic agricultural methods and master-servant relationships still prevailed. By the 1960s, however, most of Latin America was urban, not rural. For example, by then over 50 percent of the population of Argentina, Chile, Colombia, Mexico, Uruguay, and Venezuela resided in urban centers. Furthermore, a large part of Latin America, in terms of area and population, was urban dominated. And it was in countries controlled by urban-situated civilians and military politicians—Brazil and Colombia are the best examples—that the Alliance made its strongest bids to prove itself and suffered its most disastrous failures. The third inference is that the obstacles to the success of the Alliance were Latin American in origin. In effect, Washington erected a colossal barrier to success when it demanded that in return for the United States input—estimated at 20 percent of the proposed total expenditure—the Latin American elites discard their traditional, deeply rooted corporatistic tendencies in favor of democratic-liberal capitalism. The leaders of the republics were willing to make that enormous concession only at a much higher price than the United States ever envisaged paying. The fourth inference, and the key one, is that achievement, if there was to be achievement, was

**109. Over the Andes**
Bill Mauldin, *St. Louis Post-Dispatch*, 1961. © 1961. Reprinted by permission of
Bill Mauldin.

dependent on the grim determination of the United States. Over time a vast
majority of artists have chosen to relate Latin American inability to achieve at
"acceptable" levels to its racial composition; this one chose institutional grounds
on which to deny the region the chance to elevate itself.

Of the Alliance for Progress cartoons that attempted to identify where responsibility lay in Latin America, this one was remarkably discerning. Jumping Jack Kennedy's finger of guilt is pointed at landowners and industrialists, two of the three principal homegrown culprits, the other being civilian and military bureaucrats. In terms of educating the public, the cartoon is also remarkable in that its "victim" is outfitted in Western-style apparel—usually reserved for statesmen friendly to the United States—rather than the stereotypical sombrero, sarape, and buttoned-down pants.

**110. Jumping Jack**
Art Poinier, *Detroit News*, 1961. Reprinted by permission of *The News*.

The Alliance for Progress was justified to the United States taxpayer largely on the grounds that if the Latin American republics did not institute massive social reforms there was no alternative to their experiencing violent revolution which communist agents would exploit. Inherent in that projection was the implication that revolution would see the United States inevitably ending up on the losing side. This cartoon accepts the reform-or-revolution thesis and seemingly gives the advantage to revolution. That position proved wrong, as there were good reasons at the time to believe it would. Aside from the fact that Latin America is far too diverse to be generalized about, there were at least two considerations in favor of a course somewhere between reform and widespread armed rebellion. In the first place, the elites knew better than anyone else the cost to them of losing political control, and throughout the century they had guarded against that possibility by exhibiting just enough flexibility to co-opt emergent urban groups as soon as they entered the political arena. It was reasonable to assume that they would not abandon readily a tactic that had succeeded in every case except Cuba. In the second place, if co-optation somehow failed and it came down to the use of violence, not only did the traditional elites have an overwhelming advantage in weapons and organization, but, furthermore, their military arm, including in many cases the police, alerted by the recent Cuban experience, had begun training in the most up-to-date counterinsurgency strategies to be found anywhere in the Western world. Co-optation and dominance in the exercise of violence may not—should not—be sufficient to keep the privileged groups indefinitely in power, but they have proved remarkably effective to date.

**111. The Race to the Rancho**

Herblock, *Washington Post*, January 7, 1962. Copyright 1962 by Herblock in the *Washington Post*. Reprinted by permission of Herblock Cartoons.

This is one of the more striking of the cartoons that use the rich-or-poor approach to social dissonance, thereby making revolution strictly a derivative of the economic condition.

Latin America once was polarized into the extremely wealthy and the extremely impoverished, but by 1962 that was no longer so true. The condition persisted in most rural settings, but in the metropolitan centers there were numerous and large intermediate groups whose interests converged at some points and diverged at others, but having in common little to gain from violence. Those intermediate groups were by the early 1960s key factors in the social-political drama. It was in considerable part because large segments of the middle refused to break with the top that those at the bottom were denied through the revolutionary processes, thereby confounding those who predicted that Latin America had no alternative but to accept radical solutions to its social problems.

**112. —And His Father Lives Up There**
Herblock, *Washington Post*, February 11, 1962. Reprinted from *Straight Herblock* (Simon & Schuster, 1964) by permission of Herblock Cartoons.

This artist seems to have placed responsibility for the success or failure of social-economic programs where it belonged, on the peoples and governments of the republics. The artist thus avoided contributing to the commonly held impression that the United States input under the Alliance for Progress was the critical variable in the process of change. What he did not avoid in making his point was the reform-or-revolution dichotomy and reliance on the sombreroed, dozing figure, one of the more overused stereotypical images of Latin America.

**113. For Some, No Siesta**
Roy B. Justus, *Minneapolis Star*, 1962. Copyright 1962, Minneapolis Star and Tribune Company. Reprinted by permission.

This cartoon is remarkable for its treatment of the Latin American situation as of 1962. It identified Argentina as the hot spot. There, thirty-five coups against civilian President Arturo Frondizi had just culminated in a successful one engineered by the armed forces. The cartoon holds the elites—rural and urban—collectively responsible for the continuing resistance to reform. It puts the Alliance for Progress in proper perspective. It outfits the central Argentine figure in a stylized, if traditional, costume of his own country. The "hopes for true democracy" were, of course, United States rhetoric.

**114. What Volcanoes? I See No Volcanoes!**
Richard Q. Yardley, *Baltimore Sun*, 1962. Reprinted by permission of Richard Q. Yardley.

Washington was convinced during the early stages of the Alliance for Progress that the containment of Castroism should be the hemisphere's number-one objective. The leadership of the republics in essence argued, for what it was worth in dollars, that the containment of poverty and unrest should receive top attention. The popular elements were not consulted—agreements under the Alliance being between governments—but, had they been, they would have made much the same point that is made in the caption of this cartoon. The cartoon is remarkable for its success in sharply delineating the differences dividing the Alliance's partners. It is also remarkable because the artist thought of having the impoverished speak for themselves and making their representative physically as large as "señor" Uncle Sam. The cartoon is remarkable perhaps most of all because the artist drew Uncle Sam to appear as if he were learning something from a Latin American who knew about the elites from having been stripped of his shoes, socks, shirt, and most of his pants by them.

**115. He's Not the Biggest Threat to This Hemisphere, Señor!**
Richard Q. Yardley, *Baltimore Sun*, 1962. Reprinted by permission of Richard Q.
Yardley.

In this cartoon the artist chose a most effective means of transmitting to the public a greatly oversimplified version of the social issue in Latin America. Throughout this century the sombrero has been the one unmistakable, all-purpose cartoonists' symbol for the area. Several considerations contributed to giving the sombrero that status. It has been and remains a readily recognizable item of apparel in Mexico, the area best known to the average United States citizen. As a medium of expression, the sombrero is benign, suggesting neither a determined will nor a military spirit, as did, for example, the German spiked helmet of the World War I era. It thus could be used to capture reader attention while simultaneously assuring that, despite occasional and potentially threatening eruptions in the hemisphere and underlying antipathies on both sides, the United States' security would not be threatened much by aggressive behavior on the part of the southern republics. Also, where official litany held unity and friendship to be the prevailing mood and where unofficially a paternalistic relationship, detested by most informed Latin Americans, was acknowledged to exist, a malleable, fibrous headpiece probably reflected better the United States image of Latin America's role in hemisphere affairs than would any other symbol from the cartoonist's bag.

**116. High Sierra**
Bill Mauldin, *Chicago Sun-Times*, 1963. © 1963. Reprinted by permission of Bill Mauldin.

This cartoon was prompted by the ouster of Brazilian President João Goulart and the assumption of control by a military regime which came to power without a social-economic program and unsure, at least for public purposes, of how long Brazil would "require" military leadership. The cartoon is notable because the artist isolated several specific burdens of the Brazilian worker and presented them without obvious resort to the stereotypes to which United States Americans had become accustomed. Had he added figures portraying privilege, uneven regional development, underemployment, and educational needs, he would largely have covered the spectrum of Brazil's social-economic problems.

**117. Presidents Come and Go, but We'll Not Desert You, Señor!**
William Sanders, *Kansas City Star*, 1964. Reprinted by permission of the *Kansas City Star*.

Because wealth and power in Latin America historically
have been associated with a triumvirate composed of
landholders, the hierarchy of the Catholic church, and
the military, it has been assumed that the greatest economic inequalities have occurred in the countryside.
That was generally the case throughout the nineteenth
century, although in the larger cities the gap separating
the very rich from the very poor was already wide and
expanding rapidly by 1900. In this century, power in the
more developed and populous countries has escaped the
landholders and has passed to urban-based bureaucrats
and industrialists who at any given time may or may not
be aligned with the military. And commerce, industry,
and government in the huge and sprawling urban centers
have produced greater extremes of wealth and poverty
and their attendant consequences than the rural areas
ever did. This cartoon with its jumble of worker's shan-
ties vividly records the fact of pervasive urban inequities.
"The other . . . summit" referred to in the caption was the
meeting of hemisphere chief executives held at Punte del
Este, Uruguay, in mid-April 1967, which resulted in the
Declaration of the Presidents of America concerning
economic issues.

**118. The Other Latin-American Summit**
Herblock, 1967. Reprinted from *The Herblock Gallery* (Simon & Schuster, 1968)
by permission of Herblock Cartoons.

The immediate background for this cartoon can be dated from 1975 when a renewed wave of "land invasions" by peasants put the nation on edge. More immediately, the land problem was given added heat and the peasants increased militancy in August 1976 when President Luis Echeverría declared that he would not leave office without land distribution in the rich west-coast region. As his term drew to a close, he ordered the expropriation of 250,000 acres of prime agricultural land in the Yaquí River valley of the state of Sonora from some 72 wealthy families and its distribution to 10,000 landless peasants. On November 26, thousands of peasants in the state of Sinaloa, south of Sonora and the nation's richest farming region, unwilling to trust the incoming José López Portillo administration, threatened to seize an additional 100,000 acres of private holdings. With the assumption of the presidency by López Portillo on December 1, 1976, his minister of agrarian reform declared that the government would not permit further illegal land invasions. But, in fact, another 107,000 acres were invaded. Negotiations led to compromise that satisfied neither landowners nor peasants. Thus, the artist, as had others before him, called attention to a recurring explosive issue in Mexico and in Latin America generally: namely, the failure to defend the rural masses from exploitation by large landowners, to which group should be added middle men, bankers, and national, state, and local officials.

The aside, "Pancho Villa, where are you?" in the lower left-hand corner, raises a special problem because it is not at all clear what the artist had in mind. Did he conceive of Villa as a reformer, which he was in a thoughtless, erratic way? Did the artist see Villa as a revolutionary, which he was but essentially of the traditional (Latin American) variety? And if the artist viewed Villa as a revolutionary, did he think that Mexico was ripe for a revolution even if led by an unpredictable, military-minded individual such as Villa? Or did the artist resort to Villa as evocative of past struggles or as a symbol that transcends specific historical knowledge yet can be identified by a large, impressionistically informed audience? If the latter were the case, the question posed by the cartoon might be seen as two-edged. First, what basic change, if any, has

**119. Mexican Saddle**
Patrick Oliphant, *Palo Alto Times*, December 23, 1976. © 1976 *Washington Star*.
Reprinted by permission, Los Angeles Times Syndicate.

the Mexican Revolution accomplished? And the answer would be, "a great deal."
Second, does Mexico need, or is the rural situation there dangerously courting,
another social upheaval of the kind that racked Mexico when Pancho Villa, riding
at the head of his makeshift army, was at the peak of his power and influence? And
the answer in both cases is, "no." After fifty years, landownership remains an
issue, but land can no longer pick up the slack or relieve social pressures. Today
the nation's basic problems are water shortages, income distribution, unemploy-
ment, uncontrolled population growth, and urban sprawl.

The twenty republics of Latin America suffered more than one hundred successful revolutions against established national authorities before World War I. The soldier-president was a hallowed tradition by the early twentieth century. The United States public seldom had occasion to take note of the use of force and violence as political instrumentalities by a president in uniform so long as he respected Washington's interest in his region, afforded protection to United States citizens and investments, and conducted his administration in such a way as not to invite intervention by European powers. The United States public was more likely to have called to its attention the posturing and comic-opera blending of military pomp, pageantry, and gaudy uniforms that military presidents used to impress their subjects, as in this instance. F. B. Loomis was assistant secretary of state. He was sent by President Roosevelt to investigate conditions in the Dominican Republic, and in March 1904 he recommended a United States receivership.

**120. Those Little Fellows Want to Look Out When I Toss the Ball**
William Allan Rogers, *New York Herald*, 1903.

Throughout the 1920s, Mexico teetered on the brink of anarchy as the nation struggled to recover from the most devastating civil conflict the hemisphere had ever known. A root cause of its trouble was its armed forces, too often staffed by individuals largely devoid of either military or administrative competence and without concern for their nation or their men. *Current History* of May 1929 claimed that the Mexican army had "more machiavellian morons in high places . . . than any other similar institution in the world." Being awarded a third of the national budget and nearly absolute control over funds budgeted to their divisions was insufficient to satiate their greed for wealth and power. Each presidential election was preceded by a purge, each victory by a military revolt.

The accompanying cartoon called attention to an attempted coup in early March 1929 led by a number of generals in defense of their "prerogatives" and against the recently inaugurated civilian president, Emilio Portes Gil. The coup was suppressed, as had been every other one during the decade, and some of the conspirators faced the firing squad; but the real losers, as the artist makes evident, were the Mexican people. In making his point, the artist employed an unusually wide range of stereotypes associated with Mexico and Mexicans: facial hair, sword, sombrero, serape, cactus, burro, and thatched hut.

**121. Another Popular (?) Uprising in Mexico**
    J. N. "Ding" Darling, *Des Moines Register*, 1929. Copyright, 1929, Des Moines
Register and Tribune Company. Reprinted by permission.

On June 4, 1943, the Argentine armed forces overthrew the civilian government and assumed control of the republic. It soon became apparent that decision making within the military regime resided in a highly nationalistic and pro-Axis "colonel's clique" known as the Grupo de Oficiales Unidos (GOU). By mid-1944, Juan Domingo Perón had established himself as undisputed leader of the GOU. When this cartoon appeared, Perón was on the verge of winning a presidential election and beginning what would prove to be a decade-long dictatorship whose chief supporters were the Argentine army, the *descamisados* (shirtless ones), the civilian bureaucracy, and at times the Catholic church.

Being chained to a military dictatorship was no more "The Argentine Way" than it was the way of most of the republics. In fact, over the preceding eighty years, the Argentine record of nonmilitary rule was better than any of the nations except Chile and Brazil and perhaps Uruguay. Furthermore, although in the United States there were sporadic outcries against military dictatorships, neither Washington nor the public had been notably uncomfortable living with a large majority of the presidents-generals. What attracted attention about "The Argentine Way" in 1945 was its fascistic overtones. What is unusual about this wartime cartoon is that it did not specifically associate military dictatorship in Argentina—the traditional variety of which would have been acceptable, as witnessed by the number of Latin American dictators who allied with the United States in the war—with fascism, the "unacceptable" part of such a mix.

**122. The Argentine Way**

Edmund Duffy, *Baltimore Sun*, 1945. Reprinted by permission of the A. S. Abell Company, Publisher.

No single aspect of United States hemispheric policy has generated so much heat and controversy in the United States as the one begun in 1947 (and still in operation on a reduced scale) of making available to the Latin American republics military aid in the form of equipment, maintenance, and technical advice. The policy was an early and direct outgrowth of the Cold War. It was meant to put teeth into the Inter-American Treaty of Reciprocal Assistance (the Rio Treaty) of September 2, 1947, and was approved by the United States Congress in December 1947.

Protagonists of the program justified it on the dual grounds that modernized and standardized weapons and forces throughout the hemisphere were necessary to defend against communism and that, if the United States did not provide military equipment and advice, the republics would obtain them elsewhere. Since the early 1960s, the case for Latin American military establishments as important to the hemisphere defense system has been made secondary to their value as counter-insurgency forces. The most cogent arguments of those who have opposed the military assistance programs have been that they are a form of intervention in the internal affairs of the republics and that they strengthen the power of existing dictatorial regimes, create international rivalries and jealousies, and under no conceivable circumstance can result in the establishment of armed services capable of significantly affecting the outcome of any military threat to the hemisphere from an extra-hemisphere power. Irrespective of the arguments pro and con, the principal result of the programs has been to increase the capability of the armed forces, a capability that has been used, except in Cuba and possibly in Peru, in favor of the traditional privileged elements. When the nationalized forces have remained united, they to date have had their way against armed opposition in every republic, again except Cuba.

This cartoon appeared as the military assistance programs were getting underway. The artist stripped the issue of nonessentials to present simply and compellingly the views of those who believed in the maxim that children should not be permitted to play with matches.

**123. The New Good Neighbor Policy**
Herblock, *Washington Post*, 1947. Copyright 1947 by Herblock in the *Washington Post*. Reprinted by permission of Herblock Cartoons.

Talleyrand is reported to have told Napoleon, "You can do everything with bayonets except sit on them." The civilian leadership in Latin America knows from repeated discomfiture that bayonets were not made to sit on, and the Latin American military establishment knows from prolonged experience that the unsheathed sword is an effective substitute for debate.

This remarkably simple, powerful cartoon leaves very little unsaid about one of the consequences when civilian political institutions clash with naked force. The cartoon is no less remarkable because the artist called attention to a pervasive situation in Latin America at a time when a number of Latin American experts were mistakenly interpreting an apparent lull in the game of military-civilian musical chairs as the beginning of a new era in which civilian politicians would finally triumph over politicians in military uniforms and the republics would somehow inevitably be the beneficiaries.

**124. The Uncomfortable Chair**

Don Hesse, *St. Louis Globe-Democrat*, 1956. Copyright © 1956, *St. Louis Globe-Democrat*. Reprinted with permission, Los Angeles Times Syndicate.

What the preceding cartoon said so very well about the military's ultimate prescription for removing civilian leaders from office, this equally direct one records for the armed forces' bullets-not-ballots strategy for keeping civilians out of office in the first place. The cartoon appeared at a time when democracy (i.e., institutionalized civilian rule) remained an ideal of the Alliance for Progress, but when in reality Latin America was entering upon its current cycle of military-dominant dictatorships. The cycle is now well into its second decade and only Colombia, Costa Rica, Mexico, and Venezuela remain in the civilian camp.

**125. Platform for Democracy?**
Roy B. Justus, *Minneapolis Star*, 1963. Copyright 1963, Minneapolis Star and
Tribune Company. Reprinted by permission.

A military junta overthrew Peru's President Manuel Prado y Ugarteche and annulled the June 10, 1962, elections in which Víctor Raúl Haya de la Torre's APRA party, anathema to the armed forces, had won a plurality. It is debatable whether or not "democracy" suffered a major setback as a result of the coup because Peruvian civilian regimes historically had been basically oligarchical regimes more concerned to see the military appeased than democratic processes honored and the masses served. Communism entered the cartoon primarily because of the Cold War climate. But democracy versus communism is not what the cartoon is about, for by giving his stylized Andean Indian center stage, the artist identified the ultimate victim of misgovernment that had characterized Peru's past. Few cartoons have so completely captured the essence of what power struggles have been about in those nations with large Indian populations.

**126. Alliance against Progress**
Richard Q. Yardley, *Baltimore Sun*, 1962. Reprinted by permission of Richard Q. Yardley.

President João Goulart was overthrown on March 31, 1964, and the Brazilian armed forces seized the reins of power which they have held to the present while brooking a minimum of civilian input. Goulart became a likely target for the armed forces when traditional civilian power elements rejected his programs for stimulating the lagging economy, keeping inflation within reasonable bounds, and maintaining the nation's credit standing abroad. He was doomed when he opted to by-pass established channels and go to the "people" and noncommissioned officers of the armed services, thereby giving the military chieftains a basis for charging him with seeking to set up the country for a Castro-like takeover.

This cartoon, loaded as it is with the symbolism traditionally used to reduce the Latin American "common man" to an object of helplessness and the area's armed forces to scornful unfeeling arrogance, may have aroused emotions in the United States, but it did little better to inform the public of the Brazilian reality shortly after the military usurped power. As rapid-fire reporting from Brazil made clear at the time, the generals and admirals and their anxious middle- and upper-class civilian allies had not "rescued" the nation with any thought of instituting "economic reforms" of the kind that might be of early assistance to the popular elements. On the contrary, their stated objective was to protect the traditional system until it could be made to work. Translated into political terminology, that meant suppressing the dissent and demands of groups newly mobilized by Goulart and his immediate predecessors, not talking to them. And the officers have held to their initial course: the popular elements go unconsulted, basic economic reforms postponed.

**127. Can He See Me Now?**

William H. Crawford, *New York Times*, April 19, 1964. Reprinted by permission of Newspaper Enterprise Association.

The charter of the Alliance for Progress called for reforms which, if implemented, would have amounted to major structural overhauling in the social-economic-political systems of the Latin American republics. That was asking too much of governments already confronted by nationalist movements from both the left and right, mounting social protests, and enduring civil-military differences. Between August 1961, when the republics subscribed to the Alliance for Progress, and October 1963, when this cartoon was published, seven civilian-led governments —one each in Argentina, Peru, Guatemala, Ecuador, and Honduras and two in the Dominican Republic—succumbed to military juntas. Political discord, to which the armed forces were major contributors then, proved a formidable obstacle to the success of the Alliance. In fact, about the time that this cartoon appeared, the Kennedy administration, out of a growing sense of frustration, issued a policy statement which in effect said, "Enough." The United States would work with entrenched regimes but henceforth no administration coming to power by force would benefit from the Alliance. That policy was aborted less than a year later when Washington, with unseemly haste, rushed to the aid of the Brazilian junta that toppled President Goulart and assumed power. But it bears repeating that to place the burden of responsibility for Alliance failures solely on military juntas, as this cartoon does, was unwarranted. The civilian elite's profound distrust of social-economic change within a framework of constitutional democracy shaped in Washington and the lack of enthusiasm on Capitol Hill once it became apparent that the Alliance was not providing instant answers to Latin America's problems were also factors of equal importance in setting the stage for the Alliance's demise.

**128. The Express Will Be a Trifle Late**
Roy B. Justus, *Minneapolis Star*, 1963. Copyright 1963, Minneapolis Star and
Tribune Company. Reprinted by permission.

Nelson Rockefeller, then governor of New York and collector of primitive art, at the request of President Richard Nixon, headed a fact-finding mission to Latin America in 1969. The mission made four separate trips to the area between May 11 and July 6. This cartoon appeared shortly after the delegation returned from the first tour after having visited Mexico, the Central American states, and Panama. Rockefeller is not known to have reported personally to President Nixon prior to the appearance of the cartoon. It thus can be considered a reflection of the artist's view of existing conditions. As it turned out, when the report of the mission was made public in November, it strongly recommended increased assistance to the Latin American military establishments, as bulwarks against communism. It also called attention to the area's pervasive demographic problems, but in deference to the Catholic church and certain nationalist groups, it failed to come out solidly for birth control measures.

Of the seven nations visited on the first trip, four were headed by armed forces officers—El Salvador, Honduras, Nicaragua, and Panama—and the army was the dominant political force in Guatemala. The military establishments in those countries were and remain among the most "primitive" to be found in Latin America, and essentially the same can be said of the actions of civilian elites and foreign investors in those republics. Thus, as the cartoon suggests, the armed forces continue to give a strong flavor to the "art" of the area, and the poor do continue to have children.

**129. It's Part of the Primitive Art That Still Exists!**
Hy Rosen, *Albany Times-Union*, 1969. Reprinted by permission of Hy Rosen.

On September 11, 1973, the Chilean armed forces with
the cooperation of the national police overthrew demo-
cratically elected Marxist President Salvador Allende
Gossens and set up a junta to rule the country. The junta
immediately emerged as an authoritarian regime bent on
remodeling traditional institutions and remaining in
power for a long time. The junta's violations of human
rights were brutal beyond anything the more politically
sophisticated nations of Latin America had witnessed
in at least a half century. Within ten days, arrests had
reached into the thousands and summary executions into
the hundreds. The working sectors were made to bear
the brunt of harsh economic measures designed to slow
the rate of inflation and raise production. Political parties
were banished and congress disbanded. The faculties of
the universities were purged of "leftists" and courses in
Marxism. Censorship of the press, including dispatches
sent abroad by foreign correspondents, was instituted
and rigidly enforced.

The junta's ideological fury reached such heights that
individuals burned or in other ways destroyed their private libraries for fear that they might be found to contain
materials the military regime would consider subversive.
The public burning of posters, pamphlets, and books, to
which this cartoon alludes, was yet another aspect of military authoritarianism to run amuck in Chile. The nation
had known occasional press censorship even under civilian government, but not since the mid-nineteenth century when the liberal José Lastarría's dissertation and
the radical Francisco Bilbao's political discourses were
burned had it experienced such irrationality on the part
of high government officials.

**130.** Tony Auth, *Philadelphia Inquirer*, 1973. Reprinted by permission of Tony Auth.

Violence has been an accepted feature of the political process in Latin America. Despite their seemingly endless coups and *pronunciamientos*, the national armed forces of Latin America have never enjoyed a true monopoly on the exercise of that violence. For a century after independence was won in the 1820s, private armies characteristically dominated the institutionalized forces at the local and provincial levels. They often successfully competed with them in making and unmaking national presidents and in other ways influencing domestic and international affairs. The great and powerful armies of Emiliano Zapata, Pancho Villa, and Venustiano Carranza which were assembled during the Mexican Revolution of 1910 for all intents marked the end of the personal army as a political instrumentality at the presidential level. Between World War I and World War II, the most spectacular challenge by a noninstitutionalized force came in Brazil. There, in 1930, a combination of private and provincial contingents committed to Getulio Vargas posed a sufficient threat to propel the leaders of the national military services into accepting Vargas as president as against the possible price to themselves and the nation of testing the strength and determination of his supporters on the battlefield. Less than two years later the state of São Paulo, dissatisfied with Vargas' policies and entertaining the thought of secession from Brazil, put fifty thousand troops in the field; but that time the national forces prevailed.

After World War II the challenge to the centralized services began to come from peasant bands and ideological armies, first in Colombia, Bolivia, Guatemala, Peru, and Cuba and later in the Dominican Republic, Argentina, Uruguay, and Chile. To date, except in Cuba, the national forces have prevailed.

The artist of this "nonpolitical" cartoon of 1944 made magnificent use of humor and symbolism to give poignancy to the very real and ever-present possibility for confusion arising from the presence of competing sources of political violence in the republics.

**131. In the Name of the Peasants and Peons National Party—Oh, I Beg Pardon!**
Drawing by Albert Hubbell; © 1944, 1972 The New Yorker Magazine, Inc.

# 8. CONCLUSION

The cartoons reproduced here are believed to constitute a valid visual record of the cluster of United States prejudices against the people and institutions of Latin America. They are at once striking testimony to the cultural underlay of the mainstream of Anglo American society, the concerns of that society about Latin America over the past century, and the gulf that separates the two cultures.[1] Because the cartoons have reflected the culture to which they were directed, they have of necessity been predicated variously upon pseudoscientific theories of evolution, wishful thinking or irrationalities about such amorphous concepts as "national destiny" and national interest, as well as plain and simple misunderstanding of what Latin America is and what it is about. The cartoons, therefore, should be seen as documenting states of mind in different historical eras and as caricaturing instead of inventorying hemispheric realities. Subtlety has not been one of their characteristics; on the contrary, their blows have been that of the club, not the rapier.

The illustrations appear to confirm the view that editorial cartoonists fear the public mind will not grasp anything but the obvious and that simplicity and naïvete preclude more subtle forms of satire. The artists have thus relied upon symbolism, not ideas, and have sought to mobilize support for a cause rather than to enrich debate. It is equally apparent that to the extent to which the cartoonists' symbols have appealed to readers' emotions by calling forth immediate mental and behavioral reactions, they have served to entrench stereotypical attitudes. The relatively narrow range of symbols the artists have depended upon for over a century certifies the public's responses to them and also the fact that concrete historical experiences live on in the present and continue to determine their shape and meaning. Cartoons 107 and 119, in particular, attest to the lasting quality of the symbols.

The cartoonists' lessons have been twofold. First, because of the universal beneficence of its brand of equality and individualism and the superiority of its enterprise and technology, the United States has a civilizing burden in respect to Latin America. Second, Latin Americans are inferior to the point of inspiring little respect or trust and lack the wisdom to know what is best for their own security and economic well-being or to rule themselves effectively. The instruction has taken a quite limited number of forms. Anglo-Americans have been depicted as controlling their destiny while denying Latin Americans, all of whom seem struck from the same mold, the capacity to follow such a path. The republics sometimes have been portrayed as feminine, which in our historically male-dominated society automatically cast them in dependent roles. Not unusually, before the 1930s they were pictured as children requiring the assistance and surveillance of a patient Uncle Sam, compelled to play such roles as doctor, nurse, teacher, truant officer, and doting father. Until about the same date, they often were cast as Blacks, a minority whose values as stereotyped by the dominant White community have represented the antithesis of those associated with the Puritan ethic. When portrayed as "Whites" or Mestizos, the republics have been made to handle their social and political burdens in ways that traverse the spectrum of our social and political negative universe. How Latin Americans have not been portrayed is equally enlightening. They have not been depicted as people who, like the people of the United States, have jobs, raise families, go to school, and grapple with social, economic, and political problems day after day to make their communities and their countries better places in which to live and work. The judgment that the collective symbols, labels, and metaphors scattered throughout this volume and missing from it constitute a form of reductionism appears irrefutable.

Every cartoon in this book was drawn originally for a United States reading public. This was intentional because the purpose of the study was to examine what has gone on in the minds of United States cartoonists to the exclusion of all others in that profession. I took that approach because I consider intrasocial phenomena more important than intersocietal factors for a comprehensive understanding of the sources of cultural misunderstandings. This is simply to say that, to understand others, a society must understand itself. The United States is moving in the direction of better understanding itself but still has a good distance to travel. Large parts of our public sometimes consciously but often unconsciously insist on thinking about other peoples in stereotypical forms. Until they recognize stereotypical traits in themselves, their stereotypes cannot conceivably be expunged. Likewise, until Latin American separatism and its different perspectives are appreciated and accepted, the root causes of those antag-

onisms that bedevil this hemisphere are out of the question. In the meantime, parochialism will continue to lead to a want of thought about the
requirements of the hemisphere, and while the new may challenge the
old, the new will not be victorious.

I have been quicker in pointing out gaps in understanding than I have
been in offering suggestions as to how the gaps might best be narrowed.
This is perhaps because after being over the ground so many times I am
convinced that there are no panaceas, no easy solutions, no dogmas, no
formulas, no single prescriptions that will serve all times and all places. On
the contrary, acceptable standards of international understanding and behavior require constant review. For example, and speaking figuratively,
yesterday the United States thought of Latin America as locked into a
hemisphere system engineered by Washington. Tomorrow the United
States, to be realistic, will probably have to cope with Latin America's determination to cease being merely a shadow of Washington and to go
global. There is the further possibility of such countries as Brazil, Mexico,
and, perhaps, oil-rich Venezuela becoming continent-based centers
around which their neighbors will orbit. For the United States to handle
successfully affairs of that nature will require a respect of cultural differences that has not been exhibited to date. It can be hoped that lessons
learned from finally confronting certain of our own racial-cultural problems may provide some very necessary guidelines. But one must hasten to
add that to date the consciousness of race as a basis of personal identity
seems much more difficult with which to cope than optimists have led us
to believe. Finally, to identify a weakness is a far cry from creating the emotional awareness needed to remedy it. I hope that such an acknowledg-
ment does not detract from the message the book conveys.

A case for directly linking the images and stereotypes found herein to
the behavior of United States officials and private citizens toward Latin
America probably could be made. I have not attempted to make the con-
nection on this occasion for two basic reasons. First, the influence of public opinion and the mass media upon decision-making processes as a field
of study is still in its infancy. Many of the issue areas explored by such concerned scholars as Gabriel Almond, Bernard C. Cohen, Robert Dahl, V. O.
Key, H. R. Mahood, James N. Rosenau, and Betty H. Zisley, whose works
I found most helpful, remain to be tested empirically.[2] For example, to

what sectors of the public, if any, have policy makers listened in different historical eras? To what extent do the interests and groups into which the public is divided represent so diverse and conflicting objectives that in peacetime they tend to cancel out one another? To what degree do the Anglo-Americans' values and worries that their generosity may go unrequited make them atomistic rather than corporate individuals of the kind suited to accepting international bargaining? How does the informed citizen's desire to end foreign involvements quickly keep one from maintaining pressures on those in control of public and private agencies engaged in overseas activities? To what degree does the citizen's enmity toward and ignorance of foreign cultures produce a tendency for his or her moods to gyrate between idealism and cynicism rather than to engage in sustained searches for rational responses to international issues? More specifically in reference to Latin America: in what ways, if any, has the fact that historically there has not been in the United States a Latin American pressure group with nationalist attachment to any one of the republics—of the kind that, for example, Irish-Americans, Italian-Americans, Polish-Americans, and Czech-Americans have provided their homelands—given decision makers in the Latin American area a freer hand than they would otherwise have enjoyed? Viewed from another direction, how are voting patterns reflected in the behavior of elected officials and managers of United States companies abroad? And to what extent do informed individuals —through their control of the educational systems that historically have produced the leaders of government, including those in the Departments of State, Treasury, Commerce, Agriculture, and Defense and of the mass media and multinational companies—directly or indirectly influence attitudes toward foreign peoples? My second basic reason for not attempting to relate the stereotypes to policy making, either public or private, is that, despite the importance I suspect the images may at times have had in decision making affecting the entire North and South American continents, I believe no less that major political and economic policies are necessarily multicausal in origin. And since this study relies primarily upon the data of a single input into one of several areas capable of influencing international relations, the overwhelming odds are that any conclusion drawn from it alone would be distorted. If, despite the above disclaimer, the reader wishes to consider the cartoons and the accompanying commentary in policy terms, he or she might begin by taking the two most obvious occasions in this century—the Good Neighbor Policy and the Alliance for Progress—when the United States actively but unsuccessfully sought to promote hemispheric understanding, democracy of the Anglo-American variety, and Latin American "development" and ask the question: what limitations possibly were imposed on the two programs by the kinds of responses to hemispheric affairs that the cartoons appear to invite?

# NOTES

## 1. Introduction

1. "Latin America" is a kind of intellectual shorthand used herein to refer to the Spanish-speaking republics of the Western Hemisphere plus Brazil and Haiti.
2. Although for the sake of variety I occasionally use the term "stereotype[s]," I usually employ "image[s]" because it is not so value loaded.
3. I wish to emphasize at the outset that this book is about racial, ethnic, and institutional stereotypes. I hold only that stereotypes may have been among the more important variables in certain situations and that, while at no time have they been unimportant, they never stand alone. Although I feel that "color" is a greater factor in international relations than "race," I ordinarily use the term "race," in part because it is an accepted social science term and also because, in the field of international relations, "race" is in fact most often associated with "color."
4. As distinguished from social cartoons and humorous drawings of the genre that commonly appear, for example, in the *New Yorker*.
5. The following newspapers and periodicals were consulted: *Harper's Weekly* (1916–1957), *Puck* (1877–1910), *Literary Digest* (1890–1938), *Review of Reviews* (1891–1916), *New York Times* (1940–1972), *Washington Post* (1957–1973). These were journals and periodicals of the quality read by Herbert Blumer's "effective Public"; see his "Public Opinion and Public Opinion Polling," in *Reader in Public Opinion and Communication*, ed. Bernard Berelson and Morris Janowitz, rev. ed.

(Glencoe, Ill.: Free Press, 1953), pp. 594–602.
6. I use the terms "informed public," "knowledgeable public," and "attentive public" interchangeably. I conceive of these "publics" as comprised of individuals who, because of cultural background, education, wealth, and interest in public affairs, are more likely than the public-at-large to read about and respond to problems and situations arising from an international climate. Their responses are believed to be conditioned by cultural qualities characteristic of the historically dominant, more socially and economically advantaged, White Protestant elements of the population. They are commonly acknowledged by social scientists to have greater influence on policy than the "ordinary citizen," but that judgment is essentially intuitively based. I know of no empirical study that claims to fix precisely their number or influence on policy. Gabriel Almond, in *The American People and Foreign Policy* (New York: Praeger, 1960), identifies the group by using, among other sources, the recorded observations of informed foreign visitors to the United States, mainly in the late nineteenth and early twentieth centuries. The chapter "Social Groupings and the Foreign Policy Mood," in which he uses such variables as age, sex, income, education, and regional breakdowns, is particularly suggestive. James Rosenau, in *The Attentive Public and Foreign Policy: A Theory of Growth and Some New Evidence* (Princeton: Center of International Studies, Princeton University, 1968), p. 2, reports that "by almost any quantitative standard its [the informed public's] ranks are not large," and on the follow-

ing page he states that "the varying estimates always fall within a range that does not exceed 50 per cent of the adult population." Bernard Cohen is highly skeptical of the public's influence on policy making, but, if I read him correctly, his reservations stem in large part from the fact that to date no one has developed a satisfactory methodology for measuring the how, why, or when of that influence; see Bernard C. Cohen, *The Public's Impact on Foreign Policy* (Boston: Little, Brown and Co., 1973). My conception of the "informed public" conforms in the main to Ernest R. May's in chap. 2 of *American Imperialism: A Speculative Essay* (New York: Atheneum, 1968) and for much the same reasons: namely, that interest in foreign affairs must be fed by a steady flow of information of an international nature available primarily in urban periodicals and magazines of relatively large circulation. Rural dwellers historically have had very limited access to foreign affairs information except through religious journals, clergymen, and an occasional politician. See also Kenneth P. Adler and Davis Bobrow who, in "Interest and Influence in Foreign Affairs," *Public Opinion Quarterly* 20 (Spring 1956): 89–101, identify leadership types in a midwestern suburb as "highly educated, wealthy, Protestant and 'Anglo-Saxon.'"

7. See H. C. J. Duijker and N. H. Fridja, *National Character and National Stereotypes: A Trend Report for the International Union of Social Psychology* (Amsterdam: North Holland Publishing Co., 1960), especially chaps. 7 and 8, which not only discuss national character but also contain extensive bibliographies.

8. I use the terms "policy making" and "decision making" interchangeably. Richard R. Brody, in "Citizen Participation in Foreign Affairs," *Civis Mundi* 4 (1971): 1–8, makes a distinction between the two that seems valid for his purposes but unnecessary within the context of this study.

9. The term "prejudice" may have positive connotations (as, for example, the United States' prejudice in favor of Great Britain during the two great wars) or negative ones. In this volume, the term will be used solely to refer to the sets of negative attitudes which are assumed to cause, support, or justify discrimination against a socially defined group, i.e., Latin Americans or a person or institution associated with that group. Prejudice appears in varying degrees of extremism. The Preamble of the Constitution of UNESCO, with reference to prejudice in its more devastating form, declares that it, along with ignorance, was a major factor in bringing about World War II.

10. Numerous authors make the point that "race" and/or "color" continue to govern much human behavior and continue to figure in current international affairs. Harold R. Isaacs, "Group Identity and Political Change: The Role of Color and Physical Characteristics," *Daedalus* 104 (Spring 1967): 353–375, provides a well-balanced general discussion of "race" in international affairs. Few studies place as much emphasis on race in international relations as does Robert S. Browne's *Race Relations in International Affairs* (Washington, D.C.: Public Affairs Press, 1961). See also the thoughtful analytical study of Akira Iriye, *Across the Pacific: An Inner History of American-East Asian Relations* (New York: Harcourt, Brace & World, 1967).

11. See William G. Rogers, *Mightier Than the Sword: Cartoons, Caricature, Social Comment* (New York: Harcourt, Brace & World, 1969), p. ix.

12. Hans Schmidt, *The United States Occupation of Haiti, 1915–1934* (New Brunswick, N.J.: Rutgers University Press, 1971), p. 232.

13. *New York Times*, July 14, 1964.

14. Walter LaFeber, *The New Empire: An Interpretation of American Expansion, 1860–1898* (Ithaca: Cornell University Press, 1963), places the stress on the need of agriculture and industry for new materials. Frederick Jackson Turner's warning that the free land frontier no longer existed to siphon off popular discontent was an added factor in the development of Washington's attitudes toward both economic and territorial expansion after 1890.

15. For a detailed development of an essentially similar view of hemispheric economic relations prior to and during World War II, see David Green, *The Containment of a Continent: A History of the Myths and Realities of the Good Neighbor Policy* (Chicago: Quadrangle Books, 1971).

16. For a brief but thoughtful discussion of the influence of nationalism on foreign investment, see Joseph Grunewald, "Foreign Private Investment: The Challenge of Latin American Nationalism," *Virginia Journal of International Law* 11, no. 2 (March 1971): 228–245. See Julio Cotler and Richard R. Fagen, eds., *Latin America and the United States: The Changing Political Realities* (Stanford: Stanford University Press, 1974), for a strongly pro–Latin American and anti–United States presentation of the issues raised by nationalism.

17. For a very ably developed summary of the derivation, pro and con arguments, and historiography of the legend, see the introduction to Charles Gibson, *The Black Legend: Anti-Spanish Attitudes in the Old World and the New* (New York: Knopf, 1971). Although the Black Legend was at times extended to include the Portuguese, the fact is that they for the most part escaped the harshest judgments directed against Spaniards and their culture.

18. Corruption in a variety of forms is a common theme in Glen Caudill Dealy, *The Public Man: An Interpretation of Latin America and Other Catholic Countries* (Amherst: University of Massachusetts Press, 1977).

19. See Gibson, *The Black Legend*.

20. The United States view of Spanish conduct in Cuba during the last years of its rule can be found in numerous studies. David Healy, *U.S. Expansionism: The Imperialist Urge in the 1890s* (Madison: University of Wisconsin Press, 1970), provides a reasoned account of the Cuban situation as seen from the United States. By far the best study of public opinion of conditions in Cuba during the 1890s is Gerald F. Linderman, *The Mirror of War: American Society and the Spanish-American War* (Ann Arbor: University of Michigan Press, 1974).

21. Henry F. May, *The Enlightenment in America* (New York: Oxford University Press, 1976), p. 276.

22. The term Creole refers to individuals born in the New World of Iberian parentage.

23. Arthur P. Whitaker, *The United States and the Independence of Latin America, 1800–1830* (New York: W. W. Norton & Co., 1964), p. 183.

24. See, for example, John M. Forbes, Chargé d'Affaires to John Quincy Adams, Secretary of State, Buenos Aires, July 10, 1822, in William R. Manning, ed., *Diplomatic Correspondence of the Latin American Nations*, 3 vols. (New York: Oxford University Press, 1925), I, 606. The forty-niners who opted for the sea route to California were impressed with the women of Chile's more privi-

leged elements; see John J. Johnson, "Talcahuano and Concepcion as Seen by the Forty-Niners," *Hispanic American Historical Review* 26, no. 2 (May 1946): 251–262. Leonard Pitt found that the women of early California were quite respected by Anglo-Americans; see his *The Decline of the Californios: A Social History of the Spanish Speaking Californian, 1846–1890* (Berkeley: University of California Press, 1970). Kevin Starr confirms Pitt's view; see his *Americans and the California Dream, 1850–1915* (New York: Oxford University Press, 1973). To my knowledge, the most competent discussion of Anglo attitudes toward Mexican women in Texas prior to its annexation to the United States is to be found in James E. Crisp, "Anglo-Texan Attitudes toward the Mexican, 1821–1845," Ph.D. dissertation, Yale University, 1976.

25. Harry Bernstein, *Making an Inter-American Mind* (Gainesville: University of Florida Press, 1961), discusses in some detail early intellectual exchanges between North and South America.

26. Stow Persons, *American Minds: A History of Ideas* (New York: Holt, 1958), p. 80.

27. See Bernstein, *Making an Inter-American Mind*, p. 2.

28. May, *The Enlightenment*, p. 308.

29. Frederick Merk, *Manifest Destiny and Mission in American History* (New York: Vintage Books, 1963), p. 265. See also Robert F. Berkhofer, Jr., *The White Man's Indian from Columbus to the Present* (New York: Knopf, 1978), p. 154; idem, *Salvation and the Savage: An Analysis of Protestant Missions and Indian Response, 1787–1862* (Lexington: University of Kentucky Press, 1965), p. 7; and Persons, *American Minds*, p. 158.

30. Gary B. Nash, "Red, White and Black: The Origins of Racism in Colonial America," in *The Great Fear: Race in the Mind of America*, ed. Gary B. Nash and Richard Weiss (New York: Holt, Rhinehart and Winston, 1970), pp. 7–8, 19.

31. See Nancy B. Black and Bette S. Weidman, *White on Red: Images of the American Indian* (Port Washington, N.Y.: Kennikat Press, 1976), p. 135; Ronald N. Satz, *American Indian Policy in the Jacksonian Era* (Lincoln: University of Nebraska Press, 1975), pp. 40–44; and Francis Paul Brucha, ed., *Americanizing the American Indians* (Cambridge: Harvard University Press, 1973).

32. Merk, *Manifest Destiny*, pp. 157, 216.

33. See Carl N. Degler, *Neither Black nor White: Slavery and Race Relations in Brazil and the United States* (New York: Macmillan Co., 1971), and David Brion Davis, *The Problem of Slavery in Western Culture* (Ithaca: Cornell University Press, 1969), for well-argued discussions of the role of the Mulatto in Anglo-American society, including, in this case, Canada.

34. Winthrop D. Jordan, *White over Black: American Attitudes toward the Negro, 1550–1812* (Baltimore: Penguin Books, 1969), pp. 10–12.

35. Winthrop D. Jordan, *The White Man's Burden: Historical Origins of Racism in the United States* (New York: Oxford University Press, 1974), p. 170.

36. The influence of Morton and his disciples on racist thinking in the United States is covered both well and interestingly in William R. Stanton, *The Leopard's Spots: Scientific Attitudes towards Race in America, 1815–1859* (Chicago: University of Chicago Press, 1960).

37. "Racism" is used here to mean a generalized set of stereotypes of a high

degree of consistency, including emotional reactions to race names, a belief in typical characteristics associated with race names, and either conscious or unconscious evaluations of such traits. This definition is from Daniel Katz and Kenneth Braly, "Verbal Stereotypes and Racial Prejudice," in *Readings in Social Psychology*, ed. Eleanor E. Maccoby, 3d ed. (New York: Holt, Rinehart and Winston, 1958), pp. 40–46.

38. George M. Fredrickson, *The Black Image in the White Mind* (New York: Harper and Row, 1971), p. 235.

39. Berkhofer, *The White Man's Indian*, pp. 55–62; Stanton, *The Leopard's Spots*, p. 41 and following.

40. Ernest W. Lefever, "Moralism and U.S. Foreign Policy," *Orbis* 16, no. 2 (Summer 1972): 396–410. For a more general discussion, see Paul Seabury, "Racial Problems and American Foreign Policy," in *Racial Influences on American Foreign Policy*, ed. George W. Shepherd, Jr. (New York: Basic Books, 1970), pp. 60–78.

41. Bryce Wood, *The Making of the Good Neighbor Policy* (New York: Columbia University Press, 1961), p. 5.

42. Edward A. Ross, "The Causes of Race Superiority," *Annals of the American Academy of Political and Social Science* 18 (1901): 65–89; idem, *The Old World in the New: The Significance of Past and Present Immigration to the American People* (New York: Century Co., 1914); idem, *South of Panama* (New York: Century Co., 1915).

43. For an official view of what were considered the less desirable attributes of the Latin American, see U.S. Department of Labor, *The Racial Problems Involved in Immigration from Latin America and the West Indies to the United States*, a report submitted to the Secretary of Labor by Robert F. Foerster (Washington, D.C.: Government Printing Office, 1925), esp. p. 57. Two decades earlier, John R. Commons, director of the American Bureau of Industrial Research, who was highly instrumental in shaping the course of labor history for many years, in his *Race and Immigrants in America* (New York: Macmillan Co., 1907), had expressed a negative view of "tropical peoples" remarkably similar to the one Foerster drew.

44. Gunnar Myrdal makes this point in the introduction to his *An American Dilemma: The Negro Problem and Modern Democracy*, 2 vols. (New York: Harper and Row, 1969), see esp. I, xlii–xliii. For evidence of increasing tolerance of Whites toward Blacks, see "A New Racial Poll," *Newsweek*, February 26, 1979. The report is based on "an updated version of the polls Harris [and Associates] did for Newsweek in 1963 and 1966. This time, Harris polled a nationwide sample of 1,673 whites and 872 blacks in October and November" of 1978.

45. Emory S. Bogardus, "The Measurement of Social Distance," in *Readings in Social Psychology*, Society for the Psychological Study of Social Issues, (New York: Henry Holt & Co., 1947), pp. 503–507.

46. See Katz and Braly, "Verbal Stereotypes." See also the similar findings of Louis L. Thurstone on the prejudices of students in the Midwest in "An Experimental Study of Nationality Preferences," *Journal of General Psychology* 1 (1928): 405–425. Richard T. Morris, in *The Two-Way Mirror: National Status in Foreign Students' Adjustment* (Minneapolis: University of Minnesota Press, 1960), established that Mexicans were still held in low regard in 1960.

47. Hadley Cantril, ed., *Public Opinion, 1935–1946* (Princeton: Princeton

University Press, 1951), p. 502.

48. *Gallup Opinion Index*, Report no. 22
(Princeton: Gallup International, February 1968), pp. 21–24. The problem of
extrapolating from such surveys is a
serious one. For example, the results of
this poll establish that, at the time it was
taken, the respondents were being influenced by a specific "anticommunism"
as well as the constant of "culture."

49. The Catholic church in Latin America
and its implications for hemispheric
relations is one area better covered in
the printed literature than in cartoons.
Because so few cartoons have dealt with
the religious issue, they receive only
incidental attention in this volume. If
the Church were to be treated in any detail, the cartoons prior to World War I
would show a very definite anti-Catholic
bias. The well-known cartoonist Thomas
Nast was particularly anti-Catholic, a
view that he expressed on occasion in
his art done for *Harper's Weekly*. After
World War I, direct cartoon attacks on
the Church as an institution are believed
to have disappeared. During the interwar years, the few cartoons dealing with
religious issues were limited almost
entirely to Mexico, and the cartoonists
held that the Church there was the victim of godless communist and socialist
political regimes, most particularly that
of Plutarco Calles. Numerous authors
have written on the United States Christian duty; see, for example, Julius W.
Pratt, *Expansionists of 1898: The
Acquisition of Hawaii and the Spanish
Islands* (Baltimore: Johns Hopkins
Press, 1936); Merk, *Manifest Destiny*;
and such religious periodicals as the
Baptist *Standard*, the Presbyterian
*Interior* and *Evangelist*, and the Congregationalist *Advance*. Pratt, *Expansionists of 1898*, has noted that many
religious journals employed social
Darwinist language.

50. For contrasting views of the Good
Neighbor Policy, its objectives, and its
accomplishments, see Wood, *The Making of the Good Neighbor Policy*, and
Green, *The Containment of a Continent*.

51. Linderman, *The Mirror of War*, provides a useful survey of how Spain has
been reported in public school textbooks. For more detailed discussion of
textbook treatment of Spanish culture
and Spanish influence in the New World,
see Ruth Miller Elson, *Guardians of
Tradition: American Schoolbooks of
the Nineteenth Century* (Lincoln: University of Nebraska Press, 1964), and
Bessie Louise Pierce, *Civic Attitudes in
American School Textbooks* (Chicago:
University of Chicago Press, 1930).

52. As noted in note 49 above, the Protestant-Catholic controversy that raged in
the United States until well into the
twentieth century is a major lacuna in
the history of hemispheric relations as
recorded in cartoons.

53. Thomas Milton Kemnitz, "The Cartoon
as a Historical Source," *Journal of Interdisciplinary History* 4, no. 1 (Summer
1973): 81–93, and W. A. Coupe, "Observations on a Theory of Political Caricature," *Comparative Studies in Society
and History* 11, no. 1 (January 1969):
79–95, are probably the best balanced
examinations of cartoons as documentary evidence. Kemnitz's article is also
rich in bibliographical references.
Coupe wrote his article in response to
Lawrence H. Streicher's "On a Theory
of Political Caricature," *Comparative
Studies in Society and History* 9, no. 4
(1967): 427–445, which in turn was
written to call attention to what Streicher considered to be theoretical prob-

lems raised by Victor Alba in his "The Mexican Revolution and the Cartoon," *Comparative Studies in Society and History* 9, no. 2 (1967): 121–136, and W. A. Coupe, "The German Cartoon and the Revolution of 1848," *Comparative Studies in Society and History* 9, no. 2 (1967): 137–167. Emory S. Bogardus, "Sociology of the Cartoon," *Sociology and Social Research* 30 (1945): 139–147, was one of the first attempts by a United States scholar to explore the evidential value of cartoons.

Useful monographic studies of cartoons include John Geipel, *The Cartoon: A Short History of Graphic Comedy and Satire* (Newton Abbot, Devon: David & Charles [Publishers], ca. 1972); Rogers, *Mightier Than the Sword*; William Murrell, *A History of American Graphic Humor, 1865–1938* (New York: Macmillan Co., 1938), and *Dick Spencer III, Editorial Cartooning* (Ames: Iowa State College Press, 1949). Ernest H. Gombrich, "The Cartoonist's Armoury," in his *Meditations on a Hobby Horse and Other Essays on the Theory of Art* (London: Phaidon Publishers, 1963), pp. 127–139, provides a brief, thoughtful, and readable discussion of the historical evolution of the cartoon and of the cartoonist's use of metaphors. Books in which cartoons are called upon to carry the burden of the argument include Allan Nevins and Frank Weitenkampf, *A Century of Political Cartoons: Caricature in the United States from 1800 to 1900, with 100 Reproductions of Cartoons* (New York: Charles Scribner's Sons, 1944); Foreign Policy Association, *A Cartoon History of the United States Foreign Policy since World War I* (New York: Vintage Books, 1968); Foreign Policy Association, *A Cartoon History of the United States Foreign Policy,*

*1776–1976* (New York: Morrow, 1975); Mary and Gordon Campbell, *The Pen, not the Sword* (Nashville, Tenn.: Aurora Publishers, 1970); and Lewis Perry Curtis, *Apes and Angels: The Irishman in Victorian Caricature* (Newton Abbot, Devon: David and Charles [Publishers], 1971).

54. Donald V. McGranahan, "Content Analysis of the Mass Media of Communications," in *Research Methods in Social Relations with Especial Reference to Prejudice*, ed. Marie Johoda et al., 2 parts (New York: Dryden Press, 1971), part 2, pp. 530–560, provides a quite useful survey of methodological studies relating to the mass media up to 1950.

55. Lewis James Davies, "Form and Content Analysis of the Cartoon as a Cultural Medium of Communication: A Sociological Study in the Popular Pictorial Arts," Ph.D. dissertation, University of Illinois, Urbana, 1960.

56. LeRoy Maurice Carl, "Meanings Evoked in Population Groups by Editorial Cartoons," Ph.D. dissertation, Syracuse University, 1967.

57. Coupe, "Observations," pp. 77–95.

58. Rogers, *Mightier Than the Sword*.

59. Scott Long, "The Political Cartoon: Journalism's Strongest Weapon," *Quill* 50, no. 11 (November 1962): 56–59.

60. Bob Eckhardt, "The 'Art' of Politics: Why the Pen Is Mightier Than the Meathook," *Lithopinion* 5 (Summer 1970): 64–71. Also, see Bogardus, "Sociology of the Cartoon," pp. 139–147.

61. See, for example, Henry Ladd Smith, "The Rise and Fall of the Political Cartoon," *Saturday Review*, May 29, 1954, p. 7, and Jack H. Bender, "The Outlook for Political Cartooning," *Journalism Quarterly* 40 (Spring 1963): 175–180.

62. Rollin Kirby, *Highlights: A Cartoon History of the Nineteen Twenties,* ed.

324 Henry B. Hoffman, with an Introduction by Walter Lippmann (New York: W. F. Payson, 1931).

63. Nevins and Weitenkampf, *A Century of Political Cartoons*, p. 15.

64. Eckhardt, "The 'Art' of Politics," pp. 64–71.

65. Stefan Kanfer, "Editorial Cartoons: Capturing the Essence," *Time*, February 3, 1975, pp. 62–63.

66. Smith, "The Rise and Fall of the Political Cartoon," p. 7. On the other hand, Kanfer, "Editorial Cartoons," speculates (his short article is devoid of empirical evidence) that during the 1960s, when public skepticism was abroad in the land, opinion cartoonists gained in popularity because of the pungency of their attacks upon what had been considered the colossal blunders in both domestic and international fields.

67. Bender, "The Outlook," pp. 175–180.

68. Coupe, "Observations," pp. 77–95.

69. Frank Whitford, "The World of the Newspaper Cartoonist," *Twentieth Century* 178, no. 1044, special issue (1970): 3–4.

70. Coupe, "Observations," p. 82, and Long, "The Political Cartoon," p. 59.

71. Whitford, "The World of the Newspaper Cartoonist."

72. Coupe, "Observations," pp. 82–84; Bender, "The Outlook," p. 175; Long, "The Political Cartoon," p. 56.

### 3. Latin America as Female

1. It must be noted that the conclusions reached by those who have dealt in depth with the changing role of women apply overwhelmingly to "White" middle- and upper-class females in urban environments. This is because, to date, the vast bulk of data has been provided by and about that group and also because, until recently, concern for working women and non-Whites attracted little attention.

### 5. The Republics as Blacks

1. George M. Frederickson, *The Black Image in the White Mind: The Debate on Afro-American Character and Destiny, 1817–1914* (New York: Harper, 1971), p. 273.

2. Ibid., p. 164, citing article by the Reverend Joseph Henry Allen of Massachusetts, "Africans in America and Their New Guardians," *Christian Examiner* 232 (July 1862): 114–116.

### 6. The Latin American Nations as Non-Black Males

1. *Albuquerque Journal*, March 19, 1979.

### 8. Conclusion

1. Allen L. Woll, in *The Latin Image in American Films* (Los Angeles: Latin American Center Publications, 1977), reaches conclusions quite similar to mine, including the staying power of stereotypes, such as the childishness of Latin Americans generally and the powerlessness of Latin American males. Woll also notes that in periods of stress (he uses World War II as his principal example) the image of the Latin American improves, but with the return to normalcy producers began to reinstate the traditional filmic stereotypes.

2. Almond, *The American People and Foreign Policy*; Cohen, *The Public's Impact on Foreign Policy*; Robert Alan Dahl, *A Preface to Democratic Theory* (Chicago: University of Chicago Press, 1967); Valdimer O. Key, Jr., *Public Opinion and American Democracy*

(New York: Knopf, 1961); H. R. Mahood, ed., *Pressure Groups in American Politics* (New York: Scribner, 1967); Rosenau, *The Attentive Public and Foreign Policy*; idem, ed., *Domestic Sources of Foreign Policy* (New York: Free Press, 1967); idem, *Race in International Politics; A Dialogue in Five Parts* (Denver: University of Denver Press, 1970); Betty H. Zisk, ed., *American Political* *Interest Groups: Readings in Theory and Research* (Belmont, Calif.: Wadsworth Publishing Co., 1969). For the best discussion of the backgrounds of foreign service personnel, see Warren Frederick Ilchman, *Professional Diplomacy in the United States, 1779–1939: A Study in Administrative History* (Chicago: University of Chicago Press, 1961).

# INDEX

(Note: A boldface number indicates a reference to a cartoon on that page.)

ABC powers, 56, 58, 228
Aguinaldo, Emilio, 216; **217**
Alexis, Pierre Nord, 202
Allende Gossens, Salvador, 306
Alley, Cal, 155
Alliance for Progress, 20, 68, 70, 112, 242, 244, 246, 250, 257–258, 264, 266, 268, 272, 274, 276, 302; Latin American criticism of, 114; **245, 247, 251, 267, 275, 299, 303**
APRA, 298
Argentina, 78, 228, 272, 290; **35, 41, 43, 53, 79, 275, 291**
Auth, Tony, 307

Barclay, McKee, 141
Barnett, ———, 261
Bartholomew, Charles L. "Bart," 41, 49, 51, 55, 57, 101
Bellew, Frank, 77
Berryman, Clifford, 187, 201
"Big Stick" policy. *See* Roosevelt, Theodore: Big Stick policy of
Black Legend, 10–11
Blacks: and pseudo science, 16; as scapegoats, 15; U.S. images of, 16; **173**
Block, Herbert L. *See* Herblock
Bogardus, Emory S., 18
Bolivia, **43**
Bonilla, Policarpo, 136
Bowman, R. C., 209
Brazil, 214, 228, 280, 300; **35, 41, 43, 53, 79, 215, 281, 301**
Bryan, William Jennings, 74
Bush, C. G., 85, 185

Calles, Plutarco Elías, 152, 206, 230
CARE, 19
Cargill, ———, 105
Carl, LeRoy Maurice, 22
Carnegie, Andrew, 52; **53**
Carranza, Venustiano, 100, 146, 242, 260

Carter, ———, 139
Carter, Jimmy, 254; **255**
Cartoonists: influence of, 311; and interest in Latin America, 26–27; as opinion makers, 25
Cartoons: as documentary source, 21–22, 25–26
Castro, Cipriano, 192, 194, 196, 222; **195, 197, 223**
Castro, Fidel, 112, 236, 240, 248, 264; **113, 241**
Catholic church, 11, 19–20; avoidance of, by cartoonists, 27; and economic retardation, 20
Catholicism. *See* Catholic church
Central American republics: and recognition pacts, 60; **47, 51**
Chamorro, Emiliano, 206, 230
Chicago, **233**
Chile, 228, 306; **35, 41, 43, 53, 79, 307**
Civilian vs. military rule, 296, 302
Clayton-Bulwer Treaty (1850), 36
Colombia, 176, 178, 180, 220; **43, 53, 181, 193, 221**
Columbia, Miss., 32; **33, 79, 89**
Columbus Memorial Library, 52
Communism, 231, 236, 298, 304; U.S. reaction to, 206
Coolidge, Calvin, 230, 234
Cory, J. Campbell, 161
Costa Rica, **43**
Coupe, W. A., 23–24
Crawford, William H., 69, 301
Creoles, 11, 12
Crowder, Enoch H., 150
Cuba, 80, 82, 86, 88, 90, 92, 94, 122, 124, 126, 128, 130, 132, 134, 142, 150, 164, 166, 168, 170, 216, 228, 240; **217, 241, 243, 247, 275**; as Black, **161, 163, 165, 167, 169, 171, 209**; as child, **121, 123, 125, 127, 129, 131, 133, 135, 143, 149, 151, 161, 163**; as

328     female, **79**, **81**, **83**, **85**, **87**, **89**, **91**, **93**, **95**

Cultural assumptions: role of, in hemisphere relations, 9

Cultural similarities: of U.S. and Latin America, 13–14

Cutting, A. K., 212

Darling, J. N. "Ding," 24, 65, 289

Davenport, Homer, 37

Davies, Lewis James, 22

Democracy, 20

Díaz, Adolfo, 140, 206, 230

Díaz, Porfirio, 46, 52, 98, 136, 218, 224, 260; **99**, **219**

Dobbins, Jim, 239

Dominican Republic, 64, 182, 184, 186, 188, 190, 202, 228, 286; **183**, **185**, **187**, **189**, **191**

Donahey, James, 143, 167, 225

Doyle, Jerry, 107

Duffy E., 291

Dutch West Indies, 42

Echeverría, Luis, 284

Eckhardt, Bob, 23–24

Economic issues: role of, in hemisphere relations, 6–7

Ecuador, **35**, **43**

Eisenhower, Dwight D., 110, 238

El Salvador, 198; **43**, **199**

England. *See* Great Britain

Enright, Walter, 147, 229

Estrada Palma, Tomás, 124, 128, 130

Evans, W. L., 125, 179

Feminism. *See* Women

Feudalism in Latin America, 264

Ford, Gerald, 24

Fox, Craig, 207

Frondizi, Arturo, 274

Gale, ———, 233

Gallup poll, 19

Germany, 42, 48, 182, 242; **43**, **49**

Gómez, José, Miguel, 142

Gómez, Juan Vicente, 196, 228

Gómez y Báez, Máximo, 216; **217**

Good Neighbor Policy, 20, 100, 154, 234; **67**, **247**

Goulart, João, 280, 300, 302

Great Britain, **43**, **75**, **77**, **163**

Guatemala, 136, 138, 198; **43**, **137**, **139**, **199**, **275**

Haiti, 144, 202, 204, 228; **145**, **203**, **205**

Hanny, ———, 205

Hawaii, **121**, **163**, **173**, **217**

Hay, John, 186

Haya de la Torre, Raúl, 298

Hay-Bunau-Varilla Treaty (1904), 178

Hay-Pauncefote Treaty (1901), 36, 96

Herblock, 249, 269, 271, 283, 293

Herrán, Tomás, 220

Hesse, Don, 295

Heureaux, Ulíses, 182

Honduras, 198, 200; **43**, **61**, **137**, **199**, **201**

Hoover, Herbert, 234; good will tour of, to Latin America, 108; **109**

Hubbell, Albert, 309

Huerta, Victoriano, 56, 146, 224, 262; **263**

Hughes, Charles Evans, 64; **65**

Hutton, Hugh, 67

Imperialism, U.S., 120, 160, 162, 174

Indians: in Peru, 298; in U.S., nostalgia for, 15

Inter-American Treaty of Reciprocal Assistance, 292

International Conference of American States: First (1889), 38; Third (1906), 46; Fifth (1923), 102; Sixth (1928), 64, 106

Ireland, William "Billy," 123, 227, 231

Isle of Pines, 172; **173**

Isthmian canal, 96, 220

Johnson, Lyndon B., 246, 248, 264; **247**

Juárez, Benito, 76

Justus, Roy B., 273, 297, 303

Kellogg, Frank B., 152, 206, 230; **153**
Kemble, ———, 263
Kennedy, John F., 68, 112, 250, 264, 266; **267**
Keppler, Joseph, 79
King, ———, 145
Kirby, Rollin, 23

Ladrones, Los, **163**
Latin America: debt defaults in, 40; and U.S. sphere of interest, 42; **69, 103, 107, 109, 113, 115, 235, 237, 239, 245, 247, 249, 253, 265, 267, 269, 271, 273, 277, 279, 283, 285, 305, 309.** *See also* South America
Latin America and U.S.: cultural similarities and dissimilarities of, 29
Leip, ———, 171
Levering, Albert, 35
Lindbergh, Charles A., 62; mission of, to Latin America, 104; **105, 155**
Lippmann, Walter, 23
Long, Scott, 23
Loomis, F. B., 286
López Portillo, José, 254, 284; **255**
Low, David, 25

McCutcheon, John T., 63, 149
McKinley, William, 160, 170, 218; and Spain, 86
Madero, Francisco, 56, 224
Madriz, José, 140
Magoon, Charles E., 136
Manifest destiny, 14
Mao Tse-tung, **253**
Mauldin, William (Bill), 71, 245, 265, 279
May, Thomas, 131, 165, 197, 303
Menocal, Mario, 142
Mestizos. *See* Mixed races
Mexico, 56, 74, 76, 98, 100, 102, 104, 136, 138, 146, 148, 152, 206, 212, 218, 224, 226, 230, 254–255, 262, 284, 288; Constitution of 1917, 258; and Manifest Destiny, 14; Revolution of 1910, 258; **33, 35, 39, 47, 53, 57, 61,**
**75, 77, 99, 105, 137, 139, 145, 147, 149, 153, 207, 213, 219, 225, 227, 231, 261, 263, 285, 289**
Middle sectors in Latin America, 268
Militarism, 258, 259, 286–309
Military assistance, 292
Mixed races, 14–15, 210–211
Monroe Doctrine, 42, 54, 60, 62, 102; Roosevelt Corollary to, 186, 222; **35, 37, 43, 55, 63**
Morgan, Fred, 163
Morrow, Dwight W., 152
Morse, Franklin, 237
Morton, Samuel George, 16
Mulattoes. *See* Mixed races
Myrdal, Gunnar, 17

Nast, Thomas, 23, 25, 32, 33, 213
Nationalism: in Latin America, 29; and hemisphere relations, 7–9
Native Americans. *See* Indians
Nevins, Allan, 23
New Orleans and World's International Cotton Centennial Exposition (1884–85), 78; **79**
Nicaragua, 96, 106, 136, 140, 154, 200, 206, 230; **43, 97, 107, 137, 141, 149, 155, 201, 207, 231**
Nixon, Richard M., 252, 304; **253**

Obregón, Alvaro, 102
Oliphant, Patrick, 283
Organization of American States, 52, 242; **243, 247**
Osborn, ———, 137

Panama, 220; recognition of, by U.S., 176; **97, 149, 177, 179, 193**
Panama canal. *See* Isthmian canal
Pan American Exposition, Buffalo (1901), 34
Pan American Union, 52; **65**
Paraguay, 34
Patagonia, 34; **35**
Pease, ———, 235
Peb, 247

330

Perón, Juan Domingo, 290
Pershing, John J., 58, 100, 226
Peru, 298; **33**, **35**, **41**, **43**, 79, **299**
Philippines, 208; **121**, **149**, **163**, **169**, **173**, **209**
Plaschke, Paul, 61
Poinier, Art, 267
Portes Gil, Emilio, 288
Prado y Ugarteche, Manuel, 298
Prejudice: awareness of, in U.S., 20–21
Protestantism, in U.S., 20
Public opinion polls, 18–19
Puerto Rico, **121**, **127**, **161**, **163**, **173**, **217**
Punte del Este, Uruguay, 280

Racial attitudes in U.S., 10, 12, 16–17, 19, 157–158
Reciprocity, 166; in U.S.-Cuban trade relations, 92, 94
Rehse, G. W., 181, 183, 189, 193
Reynolds, ———, 75, 195
Richards, F. T., 83, 93
Rio Treaty, 292
Rockefeller, Nelson, 304
Rogers, William Allan, 45, 87, 95, 99, 219, 221, 287
Rogers, William G., 23
Rogerson, ———, 111
Roman Catholic church. *See* Catholic church
Roosevelt, Franklin D., 234; **235**
Roosevelt, Theodore, 40, 46, 134, 168, 170, 184, 186, 190, 220, 222, 286; Big Stick policy of, 40, 242; **45**, **185**, **221**, **287**
Roosevelt Corollary, 186, 222
Root, Elihu, 46
Rosen, Hy, 305
Ross, Edward, 17
Russia, **163**

Sacasa, Juan Bautista, 206
Sam, Vilbrun Guillaume, 144, 204
Sanders, William, 243, 281
Sandino, César Augusto, 154, 230, 232; **233**

Santo Domingo. *See* Dominican Republic
Santos Zelaya, José. *See* Zelaya, José Santos
Satterfield, ———, 223
Security: in hemisphere relations, 4–6, 32, 100
Seibel, Frederick O., 151
Smith, Henry Ladd, 24
Social reform, 257–258, 260–285
Sombrero as a graphic symbol, 278
South America, **49**, **51**, **57**, **101**. *See also* Latin America
Spain, 80, 84; **33**, **81**, **83**, **85**, **89**
Spaniards: U.S. image of, 10–12, 164
Sykes, ———, 103

Taft, William Howard, 50, 52, 134; **51**, **53**
Talburt, Howard M., 153
Tampico, Mexico, 228
Taylor, C. Jay, 81
Thiele, ———, 109

United States: and isolationism, 50; and presumed cultural superiority of, 12
U.S.–Latin American relations, 16

Valtman, Edmund "Ed," 115, 241, 251, 255
Venezuela, 42, 186, 192, 194, 196, 220, 228; **43**, **53**, **187**, **195**, **197**
Veracruz, Mexico, 56, 228
Villa, Pancho, 100, 146, 226, 260

Walker, ———, 177
Warren, Garnett, 47
Westerman, ———, 59, 169
Weyler, Valeriano "Butcher," 11, 84; **85**
Whitford, Frank, 24
Wilson, Woodrow, 56, 58, 74, 100, 146, 202; **59**
Women, 12, 216; as symbols, 28

Yardley, Richard Q., 275, 277, 299
Yep, Jim, 253

Zapata, Emiliano, 146, 260
Zelaya, José Santos, 136, 140, 200